P9-DVD-301

THE

David Kopay Story

THE
David Kopay Story

AN EXTRAORDINARY SELF–REVELATION

BY **David Kopay**
AND **Perry Deane Young**

 ARBOR HOUSE *New York*

AUTHOR'S NOTE AND DEDICATION

The following names in this book are fictitious: Tim Dillingham, Ted Robinson, Mary Ann Riley, Brad Furman and Bill Stiles.
Everything else is true.

Our work is dedicated to those still trapped in shame and guilt as we once were. We hope for a time when we won't have to change the names of our friends to protect their lives and jobs, when they won't have to live in fear of being identified with us or with homosexuality.

Copyright © 1977 by David Kopay and Perry Deane Young

All rights reserved, including the right of reproduction in whole or in part in any form.
Published in the United States by Arbor House Publishing Company, Inc. and in Canada by Clarke, Irwin & Co. Ltd.

Library of Congress Catalogue Card Number: 76–29229

ISBN: 0–87795–145–4

Manufactured in the United States of America

The following page constitutes an extension of the copyright page.

The authors gratefully acknowledge permission to include material from the following:

From BALL FOUR, by Jim Bouton, copyright © 1970 by Jim Bouton, originally published by World Publishing Company, used with permission of Thomas Y. Crowell Company, Publishers, New York.

From BIG BILL TILDEN: *The Triumphs and the Tragedy,* by Frank Deford, copyright © 1975, 1976 by Frank Deford, Simon & Schuster, Inc., Publishers, New York.

From COACH, A SEASON WITH LOMBARDI, by Tom Dowling, copyright © 1970 by Tom Dowling, W. W. Norton & Co., Publishers, New York.

From I CAN'T WAIT UNTIL TOMORROW . . . 'CAUSE I GET BETTER LOOKING EVERY DAY, by Joseph Namath and Dick Schaap, copyright © 1969 by Random House, Inc., Publishers, New York.

From THE JOY OF SPORTS: *End Zones, Bases, Baskets, Balls, and the Consecration of the American Spirit,* by Michael Novak, copyright © 1976 by Michael Novak, Basic Books, Inc., Publishers, New York.

From NORTH DALLAS FORTY, by Peter Gent, copyright © 1973 by Peter Gent, William Morrow & Co., Publishers, New York.

From OUT OF THEIR LEAGUE, by Dave Meggyesy, copyright © 1970 by Dave Meggyesy, Ramparts Press, Inc., Publishers, Palo Alto, California.

From SEMI-TOUGH, by Dan Jenkins, copyright © 1972 by Dan Jenkins, Atheneum Publishers, Publishers, New York.

From ON AGGRESSION, by Konrad Lorentz, copyright © 1966 by Konrad Lorentz, Harcourt, Brace, Jovanovitch, Publishers, New York.

From WINNING IS EVERYTHING AND OTHER AMERICAN MYTHS, by Thomas Tutko and William Bruns, copyright © 1976 by Thomas Tutko and William Bruns, Macmillan Company, Publishers, New York.

From "The Great American Football Ritual" by William Arenes, excerpted with permission of *Natural History* Magazine, October, 1975. Copyright © The American Museum of Natural History, 1975

Excerpted from the poem "Alumnus Football" by Grantland Rice from the book THE FINAL ANSWER AND OTHER POEMS by permission of the publisher, A. S. Barnes & Company, Inc. Copyright © 1959 by A. S. Barnes & Company, Inc.

I would like to express my appreciation to the press for its sports coverage during the years of my career, particularly to the following newspapers and writers:

Bob Brachman	AP Wirephoto
Dave Burgin	Chicago Enterprise-Record
Royal Brougham	Denver Post
Joe Falls	Detroit Free Press
George Gauer	Detroit News
Steve Guback	Green Bay, Wisconsin Press-Gazette
Earl Luebker	Los Angeles Herald-Examiner
Georg N. Meyers	Los Angeles Times
Jim Murray	The New Orleans States-Item
Lee Remmel	The Oakland Tribune
Mike Royko	The San Francisco Examiner
Lynn Rosellini	The San Francisco Chronicle
Bob Schwartzmann	The Seattle Post-Intelligencer
Morris Siegel	The Seattle Times
Darrell Wilson	Sports Log
	UPI Wire Service
	The Valley Times
	The Washington Daily News
	The Washington Evening News
	The Washington Star
	The Wisconsin State Journal

Foreword

WE started out as opposites—he the self-assured athlete, I the introvert who never made a team, became a writer instead. But the more I questioned David Kopay about his life, the more I learned about myself. Many people I know are happy to leave athletes as "jocks" because that seems to separate the rest of us from the particulars of their lives. These easy labels are a convenient way of externalizing a condition, a way of not considering it in ourselves. I should have been familiar with that process since it's the same way a number of people have tried to make my own homosexuality more exotic than it is in order to separate my life from theirs.

Once, Kopay challenged me to a game of pinball. "No way," I laughed. "I don't play any of your games." "Why?" he asked. It was a simple question—one I badgered him with for months—but one I had never really thought about. Another time, he asked me to toss a football with him and I refused with a vehemence that amazed me.

I was forced to consider the possibility that I was repressing a far more competitive spirit than those who risked actual defeat on the playing fields. I don't see that an arrogant male writer is any different in his macho poses than his counterpart in professional sports. I think there are great similarities in the success motivations that make some of us writers and others football players.

As Marianne Moore wrote of war, I had to discover what it was in me that had created and popularized the sport of football.

Our collaboration agreement for this book was preceded by several weeks of discussions. I was prepared for Kopay's good looks and outgoing personality. I was surprised to find that he was also unusually intelligent and articulate. Just by writing those words, I am admitting to certain prejudices I held about athletes. Among my friends, Kopay came to be known as a "latent intellectual."

In Kopay, I discovered a man so deeply troubled by the questions in his own life, he had arrived at interesting and important perceptions of a lot of feelings he shared with me and others. Both of us once cringed at the popular image of homosexuals as silly creatures. To us, the image—and the real people who backed up the stereotype—seemed to represent overt self-hatred. An effeminate man was mocking the best of what was male and taking on the manners of the worst of what was female. It was a long and difficult process for both of us to accept that we are part of a minority that includes "nelly fags."

For me, the process included the realization that as a child I had been (naturally?) effeminate. In later years I deliberately changed my behavior to become more "masculine," more acceptable to the larger society. I also had to examine the source of my discomfort over effeminacy in men. It was grounded in the myths that masculinity meant strength and seriousness, while femininity meant weakness and frivolity. Women, especially, have done a great deal to dispel these myths in the last ten years; and homosexuals are now in the process of doing the same thing.

While acknowledging our uneasiness around them, Kopay and I would also like to pay tribute to many of these same people who cleared the way for our own liberation through their early activism at a time when it was truly courageous. Without the history they provided, neither of us would have spoken out publicly—I in March and he in December of 1975—about our homosexuality; and this book would never have been written.

We see our homosexuality as a natural—and traditional—expression of masculine affection—whether that feeling is fulfilled by copulation or not. In many ways I was more advanced in my acceptance and awareness of my homosexuality than Kopay was of his. An exciting aspect of this book, for me, has been watching him grow, become more comfortable with himself in the process of telling me his story, of confronting the questions in cold type. I had to tell Kopay that talking about one's sexual confusion is not, in itself, any kind of cure for the ordinary problems of guilt and loneliness which are present among heterosexuals just as much as they are among homosexuals.

While neither of us is very political, we certainly do have an active interest in the gay civil rights movement. Our purpose in writing this book, however, has not been to serve up a political tract for the cause, but we do hope that it will help in creating more understanding of homosexuals and homosexuality. We believe the state laws against homosexuality will eventually be abolished—as they have been in seventeen states already—because they are laws against nature. We are not offering our lives and lifestyles as alternatives to the majority heterosexual life. All we are saying is that we exist and nothing we do in private is as unnatural as forcing a person to live as a heterosexual when he knows he is not. The societal questions come down to how humanely the people in power will deal with human beings such as David Kopay and myself.

I hope that the conflicts that form the drama in Kopay's story are fast becoming outdated. The truth is that there is still a great deal of fear and misunderstanding about homosexuals and homosexuality. Because of this we have had to fictionalize the names of five people mentioned in this book. This was not easy for us to do. Why should Kopay be put in the position of a criminal by having to mask the identity of people with whom he once shared feelings of genuine affection? The answer is simple: these people—especially professional athletes—would lose their jobs and possibly live out their lives in disgrace. This is not idle conjecture on our part. One man we describe in this book played under a $70,000 pro football contract less than ten years ago; he has reportedly since had to change his name in order to work as a monitor in a public school.

Two sometimes difficult people, Kopay and I worked not just toward a complete and honest account of his life, but also toward a lasting friendship. Our personality conflicts—my hostile mumbling, his looks that could kill—often led to violent confrontations between us. Even these we argued out before a tape recorder. Kopay was looking for answers and so was I. Kopay and I were together almost every day for nine months in the preparation of this book. Our friendship endured and I think this is a stronger book not in spite of that but because of it.

We have often been asked a question which we should answer here. We are not lovers. We have never had sex together. That is not to say I do not love and admire Kopay. I do. I could not live with a character—absent, fictional or real—for the time it takes to write a book and not love him. The alternative produces a kind of writing I will not pursue, a shallow caricature instead of a substantive portrait drawn from the inside out.

With cold detachment, however, I laid out the elements of the story in an outline for the book. The Varsity-Alumni game at the University of Washington in Seattle May 1, 1976, seemed to offer a climax, "good or bad, no matter what happens to you." That would be the first time Kopay had faced his former teammates, coaches and fans since the public acknowledgement of his homosexuality. The last chapters would also include a confrontation with every member of Kopay's family.

As the time for the game and the family confrontations approached, I began to worry for Kopay—not as a subject but as someone I cared about. His father's threat to kill him if he saw him again could have been just talk in a moment of anger, but there was no way I could know that. The very structure of this book might well be putting Kopay's life in danger. A friend whispered to me: "I hope some nut doesn't take a shot at him during that game"—which it occurred to me was the plot of the novel, *The Front Runner:* The young runner publicly announces his homosexuality and is then assassinated as he nears the finish line in the Olympic games. Patricia Nell Warren, the author of that book, inscribed a copy for Kopay: "For the real-life front runner."

Once we made the commitment to each other to do the book, we agreed that Kopay had to go through with all of these confrontations. And, as I was forever telling him, "not just for the book."

In many ways Kopay's liberation speaks to the liberation of every person. The struggles he went through finding his true sexual identity are only more extreme in their details because of all he represented as a professional athlete. The arranged meetings with his former teammates and fans, friends and family thus in a sense became confrontations with The Church, The Family, The Society.

I had no idea how complex Kopay's story was, so we began with wide-ranging interviews that would often stray into various episodes not connected by time or geography. However, we have arranged this book—after the first section—in chronological order because this seemed to be the most coherent way of presenting the story.

We spent four-to-six hours a day for three months doing the main interviews from which this material is drawn. We conversed and argued over it for more than nine months. Although the third-person portions are mainly my work, there is not one word printed here which Kopay and I did not discuss—sometimes twenty and thirty times.

When I started typing the actual manuscript, Kopay moved a desk in beside mine and that's how we worked—word for word, line by line, side by side.

Although this is a serious story—painful for Kopay to relate and difficult for me to write, there were some wonderful moments of pure fun and real laughter. Like the running back in *Semi-Tough*, Kopay had to have his ball scores every morning. That was the reason we couldn't take advantage of a house, rent-free, in the mountains up from the Costa del Sol in Spain. One morning, Kopay almost shouted across the breakfast table: "Hey, Perry, the Dodgers won ten in a row!" I said, "Oh?" He said: "You don't even care!" We laughed like schoolboys.

We made fun of each other—about me and my damned books, him and his daily exercises. I took on all of the typing chores. For Kopay's thirty-fourth birthday I presented him with a bright red T-shirt lettered: "I CAN TYPE, BUT THANK GOD I DON'T HAVE TO."

With the first warm days of early spring in Washington, D.C., we found a picnic table in a small park at the edge of Georgetown and that is where we did our interviews. Kopay would sit there—his shirt off if the weather suited—and I would ask the questions. One day after an especially grueling session about his relationship with his older brother, Kopay put his head down on the table and cried. "When is it not going to be so emotional?" he asked.

"I can't answer that," I said, "but that's what makes this an important story."

PERRY DEANE YOUNG
Washington, D.C.

One

THAT Tuesday, December 9, 1975, David Kopay had all the appearances of a young man with everything our society admires. He looked far younger than his years. His six-foot-one, 205-pound body was in perfect athletic condition. He moved with the tense agility of a well-trained racehorse. He was a man's man, a glamorous California-tanned blond who caused every lady's eye to turn as he walked into a crowded singles bar. An editor at *Playgirl* had recently asked him to pose for a centerfold.

He was, in fact, thirty-three years old and within minutes of the most dramatic decision in his life as he bought that day's *Washington Star* to read over breakfast in a favorite place near his rented room on Capitol Hill in Washington, D.C.

Despite his exceptional appearance and an impressive football career—co-captain of the University of Washington's 1964 Rose Bowl team and some ten years as an aggressive running back for the San Francisco Forty-Niners, the Detroit Lions, the Washington Redskins, the New Orleans Saints and the Green Bay Packers—David Kopay was not a very happy man. He had tried with only half-hearted interest to organize a business selling English pub-style mirrors decorated with football graphics.

Kopay was caught in a lie between the masculine myth he so beautifully personified in public and the private reality of his life. His anxiety was so intense, he could actually feel the change about to happen. A few weeks earlier, he had returned to Washington, a lovely green city with the space that first allowed him to start breaking free of the myth. He knew intuitively that he was about to make a move, but he did not know exactly when or how. He only knew it had to do with the lies he had been forced to live with by a society that sometimes adores and worships its paid athletes as super-sexual gods and at other times dismisses them as simpleminded robots.

Like a novelist, Kopay recognized the drama in his experience and he had saved every scrap of information that would later remind him of the important incidents in his life. Like a true athlete, he wanted to be first—in this case, with the story of his homosexuality.

All of this only compounded his shock that morning when he bought *The Washington Star* and confronted his secret in front page banner headlines:

HOMOSEXUALS IN SPORTS/WHY GAY ATHLETES HAVE
EVERYTHING TO LOSE

Two

I COULD not believe I was reading those words. I sat there choking back laughter and tears. Homosexuality was finally being discussed openly and—something I never expected to see—on the sports page. Reporter Lynn Rosellini had interviewed more than sixty players, coaches and psychologists for the series. She stated as a fact in the first article: "Some of the biggest names in football, including at least three starting quarterbacks in the National Football League, are homosexual or bisexual."

The second article was a personal interview that began: "The hands are massive and scarred, a football player's hands . . . The former all-pro player is nervously toying with a coffee cup in a restaurant in the city where he is a member of a National Football League team . . . The fact that he enjoys having sex with men as much as with women could ruin his career. 'It's because of this all-American image,' he says bitterly. 'What's an all-American image today? Is it apple pie and gee whiz? Or is it honesty and integrity?' "

The next line of the story answered his question. The football hero had "agreed to an interview provided that he would not be identified by name, team or position."

From the description, I knew this was a man I had had sex with. He was the first professional football player I had known who was also homosexual. Our first experience seemed like what I had always hoped for in a sexual relationship. Here was another athlete who felt as I did. I was not alone. I was not crazy. But he hadn't really brought me out of my double-life because I was to learn that he had never been able to deal with his own homosexuality. He still hasn't. We used to stay up nights talking about doing a book together. He could never do it, he said, because of his family, because of his business, because of his football career. He is still afraid in a way that is embarrassing for a man of his strength and success.

That day I kept trying to call him but nobody answered his phone. Later he would never admit that he was the subject of that article, but he told me a pathetic story. When he went to his business office after the article appeared his boss said: "We don't care if you do have scarred hands, you're still our man." He sounded like a little boy grinning back for an approving pat on the head.

Not a single athlete had been willing to let his or her name be used in connection with the series on homosexuality. I kept reading that line and I thought: Well, at least I could do that. At least I can be myself.

A friend had just given me a copy of Dag Hammarskjöld's book, *Markings*. He said that Hammarskjöld himself had been homosexual. I guess because of that his words seemed to speak directly to my predicament. These lines stuck in my memory that day when I was making a decision of my own: "Life only demands from you the strength you possess. Only one feat in life is possible—not to have run away."

It was football that had brought me to this point. The coaches always told us to be honest and direct, to be forceful and assertive both on and off the field. They said football was preparing us for our lives later on. Football had put me in this place—now I had to deal directly with the subject and myself. Coach Vince Lombardi always told us backs to "run to daylight." That's exactly what I was doing that day when I reached for the phone to call Lynn Rosellini. By that time I knew there was nothing else I could do.

My hands were shaking. It was game time. The National Anthem was playing.

Three

LYNN ROSELLINI, twenty-eight, is a gentle, considerate person—the soft-spoken opposite of the traditional brash male sports fan-reporter. She is so pretty—her dark brown hair cut in a pageboy style—she had to have her phone unlisted to stop the calls after her picture appeared in *Parade* magazine.

The assignment for the series on homosexuals in sports was waiting for her the first day she went to work at *The Washington Star*. She had previously worked at *Newsday* for seven years, covering politics and general news. She was not a sports fan, did not go to games, but had always wanted to do "real people stories" about sports.

The editor who created the job for her was Dave Burgin, thirty-seven, who doesn't go to games either, explaining that he's more interested in the "sociology of sports" than he is in the ball scores. During his "long hair and mustache" days Burgin was sports editor of *The San Francisco Examiner*, where he got to know a lot of athletes who told him about the number of homosexuals in professional football. They talked about the Washington Redskins in particular because three players there were supposed to be fairly open about their homosexuality.

At first Burgin saw homosexuality among the negative aspects of competitive sports, the natural result of "autocratic martinet coaches equating failure with femininity and success with masculinity." But by the time he assigned the series, Burgin himself had changed. He had been affected by the front page news of Air Force Sergeant Leonard Matlovich challenging the military attitudes against homosexuality. Also, he believed that the widespread gay liberation move-

7

ment had created a climate where more reasonable discussions of the subject could take place in the newspapers.

Now Burgin says: "Homosexuality is a part of every phase, every facet of our society, any society. Yet sports have been thought of as a kind of heroic thing above society."

What convinced Burgin to do the series was a release sent out to sports editors from *The Advocate*, the national gay newspaper. A query from *The Advocate* about gay athletes had drawn this response from the public relations director for the Minnesota Twins, Tom Mee: "The cop-out, immoral lifestyle of the tragic misfits espoused by your publication has no place in organized athletics at any level. Your colossal gall in attempting to extend your perversion to an area of total manhood is just simply unthinkable."

"That letter summed up the whole sports attitude about sissyhood," says Burgin. In submitting Rosellini's series for a Pulitzer Prize he said: "On the sports page, this series not only had socially redeeming value—people are simply better off knowing these things—but it broke important ground in sports journalism."

By the time David Kopay arrived at the *Star* offices to meet Lynn Rosellini, people throughout the country were criticizing the series because of the anonymous sources. Wells Twombly, a sports columnist in San Francisco, wrote: "What makes the *Star*'s series so distressingly fraudulent is that it refuses to name names and deals in prurient sexual stereotype namely (wowie!) the virile jock-as-faggot." Burgin said: "That's the way some people think; they would really like to see people's lives ruined."

Rosellini had followed Kopay's career from his college days. She and her father, Albert Rosellini, who was governor of Washington from 1957 to 1965, had gone to several of the games Kopay played in, including the 1964 Rose Bowl. She and Kopay made nervous small talk about Seattle and the University of Washington as they went to a nearby Roy Rogers restaurant for coffee. She was desperate for a name to help document her three months of work on the series. Yet, she kept asking herself, Why should he trust me? Why should he go ahead with an interview?

After talking for an hour and a half, she felt that Kopay still needed reassurance so she took him back to talk with her editor. She listened as Burgin warned Kopay about the enormity of his decision. Burgin said Kopay should be aware of the possible consequences and should be absolutely certain before he agreed to use his name with the interview.

Kopay made his decision and Rosellini started taking notes. A photographer took his picture. At midnight, Kopay and Rosellini met at Jenkins Hill, a Capitol Hill singles bar. Kopay examined every word of the story—for more than two hours. Burgin called and asked where the hell the copy was. A hole was waiting for it on page one and they were two hours past the regular deadline.

Rosellini rushed back to the paper with her story. She and Burgin stayed with it all the way through the composing room to be sure no cuts were made. At 5 A.M., they watched the story in type being locked up for the presses. The sports establishment knew David Kopay and knew him well. They could no longer dismiss the information about homosexuality with another of those jokes.

Four

I REALLY wasn't prepared for the interview, but I also knew that was why I was there. My story—and, through it, the story of thousands of others still living the way I once thought I had to live—was about to become public knowledge.

Why I did it is a question that seems to bother everybody but me. I'm sure I don't have all the answers but I do know that it had to do with images—the way people see athletes and the way people see homosexuals. Of course I didn't have to talk about my sexual preference in public. Of course taking on any label is self-limiting and wrong. But that's not the point. Because of my homosexuality I can't get a job as a coach. Unless certain attitudes change there's no way for me to function in this society doing what I want to do. If some of us don't take on the oppressive labels and publicly prove them wrong, we'll stay trapped by the stereotypes for the rest of our lives.

Basically I am an honest person—maybe that comes from my religious upbringing. It has seemed to me at times in the past that I was lying just by walking down the street. People would see me and say, "Hey, you look like an athlete. What do you do?" I would say I used to play professional football. There would follow a lot of talk about the Redskins and Packers and other teams I've played for. I could just see their minds working on the same old stereotypes, which I think are just as unfair to athletes as they are to homosexuals. Being a homosexual does not mean you are a silly person; being an athlete does not mean you are a dumb jock. Homosexuals, like athletes, often have little more in common than coffee drinkers do.

I was caught between my own self-image and what I knew people were thinking about me. I know I have always been homosexual. I also know I am a very good athlete. While I was never any kind of superstar, I do have the credibility of having played ten years in the National Football League.

I kept making the teams year after year, although the coaches once told me I was too slow to make it as a running back. I loved playing. I think I was good for another two or three seasons after I was cut the last time. I loved being part of a team, part of a family. There was acceptance there based purely on what I could do. As long as I was able to play I never minded being relegated to the special teams or "suicide squads" sent in for punting, punt return, kickoff and kickoff return, field goals and extra points. I think it would be wrong for anybody to seize on some psychological interpretation of my enjoying those years on the special teams. It was not a case of the guilty homosexual relishing the extra punishment these squads took. In fact, I had no real choice. I either played on the special teams or not at all. But I was happy making my contribution even there.

Recently I've come to the conclusion that a lot of my extra drive came from the same forces that brought black athletes out of the ghettos to the forefront of professional sports. They were out to prove—among other things—that they were not inferior because of their race. I was out to prove that I was in no way less a man because I was homosexual. It is also true that during most of my athletic career the physical outlet of the game was a kind of replacement for sex in my life. My teammates nicknamed me "Psyche" because I would get so "psyched up" for the games. They also called me "Radar" because I could always find somebody to hit.

When Lynn Rosellini and I went over that first interview, the only thing I asked her to tone down were her comments about the University of Washington, where I had worked as an assistant coach one spring but was never asked back as a coach. I'd also been turned down when I applied for a job as a scout for the Seattle Seahawks.

I still look forward to my visits back to Seattle and the university. For the previous three years the annual Varsity-Alumni game in May had become my last chance actually to play the sport I devoted most of my life to. I played on the varsity team in 1962 in the first Varsity-Alumni game and—except for one year when I was in the Army Reserves—I have played in every game since then.

The game this year was to be in the new King Dome stadium and I wanted to be there. I began to worry for the first time that I might not be invited back to play. Most of my teammates knew about my homosexuality by then, but I didn't know what the coaches and university officials and fans would think of my public talk about it.

As Lynn had written it, the story implied that I should have been hired at the university but was not because of my homosexuality. If that was true I knew this prejudice wasn't restricted to the University of Washington. I was qualified to be a special teams coach or a backfield coach and I had applied for positions I knew were available on five different teams. Only Bart Starr of the Green Bay Packers acknowledged my application.

After telling about my problems getting a coaching job, the interview described my first sexual experience with another man. We were fraternity brothers and we loved each other. But we were always drunk when we had sex and the next day we could never talk about it.

I also talked about my brief marriage: "I loved her, but I was very mixed up. I'd gone through a very bad depression dealing with the problems of recognizing my sexual prefer-ence. And I kind of thought this was the way out of it." I did not mention that an analyst while I was under hypnosis had convinced me to get married. But the more time I spent on this doctor's couch—listening to him say I only liked women—the more I came to accept the fact that I truly preferred sex with men.

My apprehensions about the future came through in Lynn's interview: "Kopay worries what effect his disclosure will have on his business interests, his family and his friends. 'It's been such a difficult trip,' he says, 'and I'm sure it's just begun.' "

The next day the story was reprinted or quoted in nearly every major newspaper in the country. I put in a call to an old friend who had confessed to me about his homosexuality a few months earlier. He had been general manager for one of the NFL clubs. A man in his fifties now, he has never had sex with another person. But he finally acknowledged that his long association with football had everything to do with the sexual attraction he felt for men. The only difference between him and a lot of other coaches, owners, administrators in sports is that he is being honest about his feelings.

"How about letting me know when you're going to drop the next bomb," he said, laughing. He was nervous about my story—worried, I'm sure, about what it would mean for him and others who feel they have no choice but to stay secret about their sexual preference. But he was also very supportive of me and what I was doing—sharing, vicariously, in my liberation. Maybe what I am doing will help create some space so that people like my friend won't have to hide anymore.

My friend's laughter and support were in stark contrast to my parents' reaction. Nothing could have prepared them for what I did; nothing could have prepared me for their reaction. Apparently a reporter in Seattle had called them to get their reaction—and that was the first they knew of my talking publicly about homosexuality. I had told them four years before about my preference and they had never accepted it. That was why I hadn't called them before I did the interview. I knew they couldn't understand; I knew I had to make the decision on my own.

I had mentioned to them that I wanted to write a book someday and my mother would always say: "Over my dead body." I told myself that was more her rejection of homosexuality than it was of me. She had accepted the Catholic church's approach to sex and simply would not hear my explanations. She saw and still sees homosexuality as evil and disgusting—but, then, she sees all sex in the same way. She could only deal with it through the doctrines of the church: it is forbidden, therefore it does not exist.

When my mother called me, she was crying hysterically. "Why are you doing such a thing?" She said I had destroyed my older brother Tony's coaching career, that the reports about my homosexuality had kept him from getting the head coaching job at Oregon State. Tony had called them, saying he was a ruined man because of me.

I tried to reason with her. I said I hadn't destroyed Tony's opportunities. I said he was a very good coach and he would be judged on that basis, not on anything I had done. What's going on there, I told her, has a lot to do with why I decided to speak out. People think of homosexuality as some kind of curse. I knew it was a natural part of me—and always had been, even when I was dating Miss Washington and the Rose Bowl Queen. The problems I have experienced came from my confusion and fear over what other people would think of me as a homosexual.

"Mother," I said, "you know how hard I've tried to get back in football as a coach. Am I supposed to hide? Am I supposed to keep my mouth shut and allude to ladies everybody thinks I'm going out with? Do you want me to go ahead and lie like they want me to? That's not what I'm about."

She asked why I hadn't told them about the interview in advance. I said, "Mother, I've told you for so long and you haven't made any progress toward accepting it. You keep saying I'm not a homosexual and I know I am." "We can't even go outside the house," she said. I reminded her how friendly she and Dad were with a gay couple in the neighbor-

14

hood. She said, "That's not my son." She also said they would have to put the house—where they have lived for more than twenty-five years—up for sale and move away.

I asked about Dad's reaction and she put him on the phone. "What the hell do you think you're doing? Who the hell do you think you are?" I said, "I know who I am." He said if I were there he would kill me. He said he never wanted to see me again. I couldn't talk any more. I was crying as I hung up the phone. It seemed my parents would never overcome the attitudes about sex that kept them from dealing with my homosexuality, attitudes, I knew, that had also always kept them from being more open and loving with each other.

Otherwise I was relieved and happy about most of the response to my interviews—first in the *Star* and then in other publications and on television. Even the negative reactions confirmed the importance of my speaking out. A columnist from Milwaukee wrote about a woman who said her son had my autograph and now she wanted him to tear it up. A man quoted in that column said he always thought I swished when I was running around end. I had to laugh at that one because the coaches were always yelling at me for not having enough nifty moves.

Mike Royko of Chicago wrote in his syndicated column about a wife's spoiling her husband's game by commenting on the homosexual aspects of the sport. Johnny Carson asked Joe Namath if all this were true about homosexuality among professional football players. Namath made a camp gesture of shock and wouldn't answer the question.

Lefty Driesell, basketball coach at the University of Maryland, called up and raved at Dave Burgin: "It is beyond my comprehension that a responsible sports editor could stoop to such trash when there are so many good things to write about in sports. What about the kids who read this stuff? They're easily influenced by what they read. What are they supposed to think? That to get publicity for playing sports you have to be queer?" Reacting to Driesell's words, Jane O'Reilly, a *Star* columnist who also writes for *New York* magazine, praised Lynn Rosellini for "extending the new humanism even to the sports pages . . . Human Being, properly marketed, could even replace the present image of Mythic Masculine Hero."

Mike McCormack, then head coach of the Philadelphia Eagles, was quoted as saying: "My reaction was one of sickness. I don't know first-hand of any homosexuality and I don't know where it would fit in. I don't see any purpose to the article unless it was to get publicity for the girl." McCormack had been very friendly to me when he was an assistant coach and I was a player for the Washington Redskins. The other player quoted anonymously in the *Star* was one of McCormack's all-time favorite players. If McCormack did not know about the homosexuality or bisexuality of some of the outstanding players he has coached in Washington and in Philadelphia, he was the only man in the National Football League still ignorant of their names.

The letters to *The Washington Star* were overwhelmingly negative. The tone of most of them was that this subject should not even be in the newspapers—and certainly not on the sports pages. George Beveridge, the *Star*'s ombudsman, responded to these letters by saying that the series only showed "that professional athletes are no less human beings in this regard than the rest of us, but that the blanket of secrecy surrounding the subject has helped to perpetuate situations within the male and female pro ranks that are both tragic and absurd."

Most of the other response, though, was positive. David Susskind (who once said he would send his son to a psychiatrist if he told him he was homosexual) was understanding and supportive of me when I appeared on his show, and so was Tom Snyder on the *Tomorrow* show. Snyder's show is normally taped at 8 P.M. for broadcast later that same night. The night of March 17, 1976, I sat waiting in the control room while Snyder interviewed Jimmy Carter for what was to have been only the first half of the show. As it neared the time

16

when I was to be interviewed, Snyder interrogated Carter about laws against homosexuals as a sort of transition to my segment. By coincidence, that was a turning point in the campaign—Carter had just won the Illinois primary—so the candidate decided to stay the full hour and my portion wasn't taped until the next day. Carter was hardly what I would consider progressive in his responses to the questions. He said he was definitely against discrimination against homosexuals in employment and housing but he could not see any change in the federal laws where the employee might be a security risk because of his or her homosexuality. He offered that same old excuse for not changing the law. However, this was surely a rare time when a presidential candidate was even questioned on the subject.

A number of doctors, lawyers, professors and people in nearly every profession had announced their homosexuality and hadn't gotten nearly this much attention. I understood why I was being given this very privileged platform. I tried to speak from my own experience in a way that would have some meaning to people in my own condition, but would also help to explain our lives to those who—out of fear or ignorance—had caused us so much pain.

In the months that followed that first interview, I received several hundred letters. Only three were negative; all three came from my aunts. After an interview in *The Advocate*, my Aunt Gerry Stifter wrote: "If you have any explanation for this latest publicity stunt, please give it to your Mom and Dad. Try to consider their difficulty in understanding your position, especially when it is presented in this manner. Perhaps you will be more selective in your avenues of publicity. I wish you no harm, Dave, quite the contrary. I send this because of my love for your Mom and Dad and concern for your own well being. I say my aspiration, 'Sacred Heart of Jesus, I place my trust in thee/Sacred Heart of Jesus, protect our families,' which includes you too. I send this with tears in my eyes, for I have always held you in high regard. Sincerely, Aunt Gerry."

17

The other two came from an aunt who is a nun and another who has been principal of a public school for twenty-five years.

All of the other letters I received were statements from the closet, from people who felt trapped. They thanked me as they would a friend for helping them. The letters were from all kinds of athletes and from people in nearly every profession. Many of them said the same things I would have said ten years earlier. One of my favorites came from a young man in Delaware:

"You've got a lot of guts, buddy. My life's been torture until I saw the articles in the *Star*. I thought I was losing my mind or something. I've never had any trouble getting girl friends, but sometimes it feels like an obligation. There're some girls sometimes I think I'm really in love with, but down inside no girl has ever made me feel like I feel about some buddies of mine.

"When I looked at what people told me were homosexuals, I thought I'd be sick to my stomach. None of the guys I know are like that. The people I was told were homosexual didn't make me feel anything. They're not interested in the same things I am. I can't see any of those people being part of my life. I've always kept everything I've felt to myself. The only thing I've had to console me is that one night a good friend of mine came over to my room one night after a party. We slept together, and I knew from the way I felt it was the real thing. But after that night it was months before he'd even say more than hello to me. I was never more miserable in my life. I started spending a lot of time with a couple girls to try to forget, but it wasn't the same. I wondered if what had happened that night had just been some kind of accident. After reading those stories, I know it wasn't any accident. They showed me I wasn't losing my mind. Man, when I think what a long cruel joke it's been, I want to go out and cream somebody. There's probably a lot of guys in the same place I am who just haven't been saying what they feel. Thanks."

18

I mounted all those letters on paper and made a kind of "book of faith" out of them. Whenever I have any doubts about my decision to speak out, I turn to somebody else's story and feel reassured. Whatever my life is now, it's healthier than when I had to live with the gossip and the jokes and the lies about being masculine and being homosexual.

It has been a long and difficult journey for me. Sometimes I feel cheated for all the years I wasted in hiding. There were times when it seemed that the promise of "life, liberty and the pursuit of happiness" granted to other people would be denied me because of my sexual preference. There was a time when I felt that it would be the end of the world if people found out about my homosexuality. What I have found is that it's the beginning of a new world for me. This experience—both the highs and lows—has been like the emotions of a really good football game to me.

Five

In his recent biography of the great tennis player, *Big Bill Tilden, the Triumphs and the Tragedy,* Frank Deford—a senior writer for *Sports Illustrated*—says: Tilden's childhood reads like a textbook of circumstances liable to produce a homosexual male: the neglectful father who was devoted to another brother; the overprotective mother, warning her baby about the dirt and disease of sex."

Deford cites only one dated study as evidence for such a sweeping generalization on the cause of homosexuality. There is such substantial disagreement among professional psychologists and psychiatrists who have studied homosexuality for decades, it is curious that a writer in 1976 would attempt to reduce so complex a subject to such simplistic language. Deford's formula could just as easily apply to other segments of the population—and to the lives of such as Franklin Roosevelt and Harry Houdini, among others, who—from all reports—did not turn out to be homosexual.

There are two inherent dangers in being so quick to invoke the easy formulas regarding homosexuality. It is an inaccurate way of isolating homosexuality from the rest of society, a way of making it seem more alien than it is. While the Kinsey reports showed that only as much as five to ten per cent of the population may be homosexual, they also showed that well over half of the male population had had at least one homosexual experience. If most people do not choose to indulge in homosexual activities, they are aware that it is within their capability to do so. The confusion this sometimes brings to their lives is something they would usually prefer not to deal with—and so they tend to separate themselves and others from homosexuality with labels rather than fact. The

23

other dangerous consequence in the label itself is for the homosexual. "Homosexual" is certainly a part of one's identity, but the word does not define any man or woman totally. It can become a way of being homosexual, and nothing more. If someone says simply, "I am homosexual," many therapists today might well respond: "But what's your problem?"

It was Sigmund Freud himself who wrote an American mother that ". . . homosexuality is assuredly no advantage but it is nothing to be ashamed of, no vice, no degradation, it cannot be classified an illness . . ." (The letter is now preserved at the Kinsey Institute.) The American Psychiatric Association no longer lists homosexuality as an illness.

The childhood of David Kopay would fit Deford's formula for producing male homosexuals. However the formula also fits Kopay's older brother and younger brother, who turned out to be acceptably heterosexual.

Six

ONCE when I was eleven years old I heard my mother crying for help from the living room. I ran in to see my father choking her. I thought he was going to kill her and I started yelling, "Stop it, stop it!" I grabbed his arm and he did stop. Another time I sat up all night in the den, afraid to go to sleep because my mother said after one of their fights, "Your father might kill himself and us."

I do not remember a time in our house when there was not some kind of fight going on between my parents. Not once do I remember them exchanging any kind of love words. What I most often heard them call each other was, "You son of a bitch." I would take sides with my mother only if there were a physical threat. I blamed them both for all the noise and the tension. Because of these scenes in my childhood I will now leave a room if people start arguing.

My aunt and uncle at times suggested counseling for my parents, but my mother would always say that prayer was all they needed. They would go to church and come home to continue their fighting.

I never knew what their arguments were really about; they were just always there. Even then, I knew or sensed they couldn't be about the trivial things they were shouting at each other.

My father was thirty-two years old when he married. After one of their arguments I asked him why he got married since he had waited so long. It did not seem to me that he and my mother really loved each other, and love—according to the words of the church—was what marriage was supposed to be about. "Well," he said, "it was time." It was important, he explained, for a man to have a wife and children. It was what was expected of him. To him, that was enough of an explanation.

Both my parents were reared as strict, unquestioning Roman Catholics. They were brought up in a rigid society that offered them no real choices. They either got married or they did without sex. I believe that unnatural approach to life caused me twenty years of agony over sex. I believe it warps my parents' relationship to this day.

My parents often seemed to hate the lives imposed on them. My mother would talk resentfully of birth control. It had not been an option in her life. I later learned that the absence of sex because of a fear of pregnancy kept my parents from having a normal, healthy relationship and surely contributed to their outbursts of unreasonable violence.

On more than one occasion this violence was turned on me. Once I was wrongly blamed for carving a big "K" on the back of a new rosewood buffet my parents had bought. My father chased me, swinging his belt wildly and shouting, "You no good son of a bitch." He cornered me in the bathroom and kept beating me until I used a plunger to fend off his blows and ran out the door. I don't think my father really wanted to hurt me, I think his violence was the same I saw later in myself and other athletes. Our frustration—in many cases over sex—caused us to strike out blindly, my father at a defenseless child, myself and other athletes at other men obviously weaker than we were.

When my parents had to confront the questions posed by their children's lives—my homosexuality, my sister's divorce, one brother's marriage to a Protestant—I think they were actually jealous of the freedom we could enjoy. They resented our telling them that much of the misery in their lives had been unnecessary. Who could blame them?

My father, Anton Kopay (the name was originally Kopaytich), was born a first generation Croatian. He was proud of being Croatian, and sometimes would take us to a Croatian wedding or dinner. Both my parents loved to dance, and if ever a polka was played they would move to the center of the floor, outshining all the other couples. Even this caused arguments, though—over which one was better, over whether one was trying to outshine the other. This constant competition—always for our attention and love, it seemed— kept me torn between them.

Dad grew up in a mining town, Cherry, Illinois, but we visited it only once. We also made one visit to St. Mary's Cemetery in Chicago to visit his mother's grave. It was the only time in my childhood I ever saw my father cry. He talked some about his stepfather who forced him to drop out of school in the sixth grade to work twelve hours a day, seven days a week, in the mines, and who then took away from him all the money he earned. We saw Dad's brothers and sisters no more than a few times. He rarely talked about his family.

At eighteen Dad went into the Marines. He stood five feet eight when he went in and six feet when he came out. Being six feet tall was important to him. In fact, the only thing I ever heard him brag about was his physical condition. He would let us swing on his arm while he flexed his muscles: "Not bad for an old man," he'd say. Now at age seventy-two he weighs 185 pounds and has a thirty-four-inch waist. While in the Marines he went to Haiti, among other places, and kept a little box of snapshots of himself and his buddies that he would never let my mother throw out.

A handsome young man, he had black hair, huge strong hands and a face with big features, like mine. People called him "chief" because he looked like an Indian, an impression reinforced by his expressionless face and his silence. My friends were afraid of him, mostly because they never knew when he was angry. He would sit at a family party and never volunteer a word. He drank a few beers every day but never got drunk.

My parents met at a dance, my mother was nine years younger, headstrong and independent. Marguerite Hahn was the second of eight children. Her father was German, her mother Irish and one branch of the family French. All of them were Catholic. She was a spirited, buxom woman, proud—as she still is at age sixty-three—of her shapely legs.

My mother was the kind of girl I used to watch the nuns scold in grade school, telling them as their breasts developed to cover up, teaching them to be ashamed of their bodies. Those who didn't were accused of "getting the boys in trouble." An old pamphlet I came across that spelled out much of this was endorsed by the late Samuel Cardinal Stritch, Archbishop of Chicago: "Venuses and the rest debase and degrade and lead men to sin. There is a crusade, a crusade which started centuries ago, and that is the crusade of Our Blessed Lady among women.

"Christian modesty demands," the pamphlet said, "under pain of sin, that dress be such as to conceal and in no way emphasize the parts of the body which, if revealed or suggested, are an occasion of sin to normal individuals."

Looking back, I believe my mother had a rich sexuality and a spirit as restless as mine. I also think she repressed all that—as the church dictated—never missing a single day's mass or a Tuesday night Mother of Perpetual Help devotional or any of the special holy day services. My questioning of her beliefs in recent years have apparently caused her to become even more religious. Yet I keep recalling how she once talked about dyeing her hair blond when she was a young girl. That may sound like a simple act now, but in that strict Catholic community in Chicago where my mother was born it was outright rebellion.

My parents' marriage was caught in a cycle of poverty that offered no consolation for their other suffering. With no form of birth control they had four children they could not afford to keep in the manner expected of them in the church community. "Yes," my mother would say, "Jackie Kennedy's sister can get out of a marriage. If you've got money, you can get anything."

But if my mother often seemed extreme in her scolding, I

know it was only because of her deep desire to see her children better off than she was. I also know that the only chance of advancing herself was through us. If my father sometimes seemed a tyrant at home, I now understand it was because that was the only place where he could demand and get respect. With little education and no technical skills he was never able to get the jobs that would have provided the money my mother—and the church—demanded. He worked at the Chicago stockyards for a while, then got a job on an open streetcar. The work was cold, demeaning. I often wonder how my parents ever kept us in food, much less paid the tuition for us to go to private schools—I was a teenager before my father ever earned more than $100 a week. Nonetheless, he managed to buy a little white-frame track house in a section that in those days was in the outskirts of Chicago, with tree-lined streets, open fields—even some truck farms—and a rock quarry and two lagoons my mother wouldn't let us get near. Now it's just another part of the urban sprawl of the South Side.

I was born on Sunday, June 28, 1942, in Little Company of Mary Hospital in Chicago. "But Sunday's child has everything," as my mother would quote the rhyme. My Christian name was David, my Baptismal name Marquette (a surname from my mother's family) and my confirmation name William for my Uncle Bill Stifter, who was married to mother's sister, Gerry. Aunt Gerry was my godmother when I was baptized, and Uncle Bill was my sponsor at confirmation. A registered nurse, Aunt Gerry is a warm and caring person, the mother of eight children and my mother's best friend. Uncle Bill is a jovial German who loves to have a few drinks and tell jokes. As a child I remember seeing him make what would now be called camp gestures as he told stories about homosexuals, mixed in with other jokes about sex, about being horny.

My parents almost never joked about sex—in fact neither of them ever seriously discussed it with me at all.

I was the second of four children. Tony was the firstborn, the first of thirty-three grandchildren on my mother's side and the runner-up in a "beautiful baby" contest in Chicago. Gary and Marguerite came after me. There was such an age difference between myself and Marguerite we hardly knew each other growing up. She says she was a spoiled little girl, Dad's favorite, and she remembers that I once turned her over my knee and spanked her. I also sided with the family against her when she wanted to move out and get her own apartment. One of the main reasons she decided to get married, she says, was to get out of the house. Mother cautioned her about having sex too often, about "letting him use you." "But Mother," Marguerite would say, "did it ever occur to you that I'll be 'using' him too?" The marriage didn't last, and Marguerite got a divorce.

She did, though, discover water skiing with her husband and later became a very good snow skier. Rich Catholic girls have their tennis and golf, but until her marriage the only athletic achievement open to Marguerite was cheerleading. In learning to ski, taking some bad falls, conquering some steep turns, she began to realize she could be in control of herself. She was the one who had to pick herself up when she fell. And she saw she could do it very well.

Because of the changes in both our lives, Marguerite and I are now best friends. Sometimes we share an apartment, and people often ask if we are lovers when we go out because of our open show of affection.

Gary, the youngest son, was also the smallest as a child. He suffered from asthma and once was burned very badly. Now he looks like a football player himself, although he weighed only ninety-nine pounds when he graduated from high school. There was no kind of rivalry between myself and Gary because I knew he couldn't compete in the areas that mattered to me, and I couldn't compete in his best areas—he was a very good student, grades always at the top of his class, and the math teachers would ask me why I couldn't do as well as

Gary. I actually liked that. It meant that he was getting some recognition too.

Very early, Gary saw that any accomplishment he made would have to be outside Tony's and my world of sports. He joked about us as the "big dummies" in the family, but he also says he never had any real self-confidence until he graduated from UCLA and earned his second lieutenant's commission in the Air Force. When Gary decided to marry Charla Donahue, a Presbyterian, my mother's reaction was almost as hysterical as when I later told her I was homosexual. Gary and Charla went to a priest who told them they could be married in the church if they would sign a paper promising to raise their children as Catholics. After that, the priest said, they could forget about it. No, they decided, they were not going to begin their marriage with a lie and were married in a Protestant ceremony my mother could never accept. Once my mother called their two children "pagans," and Gary told her: "Listen, if you ever mention religion to me, you will never see me again. And I mean it." Mother never did and they are now closer than before. It seems that since my public discussions of my sexual preference, my parents have transferred the attention they once focused on me to Gary and his family. When others in the family were so shocked about my disclosure of homosexuality, Gary just said, "Whatever he does is his business. This is not going to be a problem in my life."

My older brother, Tony, was the one I ran after. He was two and a half years older and was always trying to ditch me. He seemed very strong and adventurous. He wasn't afraid of dogs or chickens or geese the way I was, he had the nerve to run when Dad would come after us with a belt. The truth is I was always very intimidated by Tony and we fought constantly, even through college. Once I got so angry at him I threw a knife, which stuck in the headboard behind him. It was the first time he ever ran from me, and I was scared because I realized I could have hurt him or worse. We shared the same bed and if I dared move over an inch on his side there would be a fight. If I touched any of his clothes that too was reason for a fight. I never really thought in terms of outrunning Tony. Even though I was taller and heavier than he was, he could always whip me in a fight. I didn't imagine there would be a time when I would overshadow Tony because I just didn't think that was possible. After all, he was already a favorite of the coach before I got to Notre Dame High School; he was a member of the University of Washington's Rose Bowl team a year before I got there.

The week I first talked about my homosexuality in public was also the week Tony was being considered for the head coaching job at Oregon State University, and he blamed me when he didn't get that job but instead was named offensive coordinator and assistant coach. Later his wife Marion would write me that Tony had cried openly in church one Sunday when the priest spoke of being more considerate of other people's lifestyles. She felt, she said, that this was a sign Tony was getting to be more compassionate in his thoughts about me. But later Tony told me, "I cannot accept your homosexuality." I can't help but believe at least part of this is his way of expressing some old resentments that had built up through the years. I did become a bigger football star than he was in college, I did go on to the pros and he did not. Today Tony is the only one of us who still lives within the church. His wife is Croatian and Catholic. He is as strict and uncompromising with his young daughter as he is with his football players—as rigid as our parents were with us.

Yes, there were negatives in the way we were brought up, but my parents were also naturally strong people with the capacity for love, even if they weren't able to express it. And if I'm able to become a loving, compassionate person that too should be credited to them.

I am only saddened that there was so little outward sign of the love among us, even though I now believe it was always there.

Seven

WHEN we lived in Chicago there was never enough money. We never had a car and we were the last people on our block to own a television set. The only money I had for the mission pot or an ice cream at school was what I took from Dad's money-changer from the streetcar. I still don't understand how he didn't notice that two or three dollars were missing every week. Maybe he thought Mother was using it for the house. All the money he earned went for food, the house and our school expenses. Even if he had wanted to go out to a bar, there was no money for it. The biggest treat I remember was Dad bringing home an extra White Castle hamburger in a little cardboard fold-out box shaped like a house.

Our house on Sawyer Avenue at 103rd Street was neat inside and out with a Sacred Heart of Jesus over the door and religious figurines and objects in every room. A jar of holy water was kept in a closet, and when it would thunder and lightning Mother would take it out and sprinkle holy water about the house for protection. Dad loved working in the yard, which included a row of lilac bushes up next to the house and a big cherry tree at the back of the yard.

My memories of Dad are chiefly of an aloof figure who was either silent or violently angry. He never called me by my first name, he never called me "son." Even now he just says "hello" to me on the phone, no name. But there was another side to him, a more loving side I like to think was always there even if he couldn't express it. Sometimes he would play the harmonica for us, or take on the voices of Br'er Rabbit and Br'er Fox as he read to us from the Uncle Remus stories. He loved to cook—gnocchis and fried chicken were his specialty, but he did most of the regular cooking too. Even during whole weeks when he and Mother weren't speaking he would still get up and fix her breakfast. Once when I had both measles and chicken pox Dad brought a mother rabbit and her new babies in a box to sit by my bed. It was one of the rare times when he showed any open affection for me, and recalling it can still make me cry.

I suppose the way we lived in Chicago was not different from the way Catholic families lived anywhere else in America. Our lives centered around St. Christina's church and my mother's family. My grandmother was a powerful woman, self-conscious about being too short to reach the kitchen shelves, fiercely independent and proud. She was very strict with her own children. Three of my mother's sisters never married—Dolores became a nun, taking the name Sister Susan; Marie became a schoolteacher and principal; Coletta was in the Women's Army Corps and later became a schoolteacher.

I was especially close to my aunts. They had their own cars and had traveled more than others in the family. When I was playing football Aunt Coletta would drive any distance to see me play. Sister Susan and her friends would also use my apartment when I was out of town. They remained close to me until I started talking about my homosexuality. For several months after, they kept the news from my grandmother.

Uncle—he was actually a great uncle—Johnny Berry was the most interesting of my relatives. He had been injured in a motorcycle accident as a young man and had a bad limp, an oozing leg wound hobbling him for the rest of his life. He was eccentric, which nobody ever called him, and lived with a retarded sister in a big old house near St. Christina's, where we went to school.

To me Uncle Johnny Berry's place was like some fantastic jungle as I opened the gates into his elaborate front yard. He had a grotto to the Blessed Mother and a fish pond and all kinds of trellises and beds of bright-colored snapdragons, sweetpeas, lilies of the valley, marigolds, zinnias and dahlias. In the backyard was a small pond for the geese and a big pen for the chickens, and he had a greenhouse on the back porch where he raised his own plants.

Inside the house was dark and musty—the lights all had lamps or chandeliers, never just a bare bulb. Every week Uncle Johnny baked cakes, pies and bread for the priest. Sometimes he would also give us something he had baked. The chairs and tables in his house were covered with doilies he had crocheted. He made scarves and bedspreads, tablecloths and knitted fringed shawls, one of which he wore all the time.

I was frightened of Uncle Johnny Berry at first. He was the only man who ever hugged or kissed me. At Christmas his living room was a child's vision of make-believe, including a miniature Austrian village he built that took up the entire room. A visit to his house was a pleasant retreat from our own, where every holiday was spoiled by those perpetual wrangles between my parents that only got worse with the "happy" seasons.

Uncle Johnny Berry was also the most creative person in our family. I couldn't identify with his knitting and crocheting, they weren't things I wanted to do, but I could identify with his appreciation of beauty, his love of cooking, gardening and caring for animals. My parents also liked to visit him— they too appreciated his differences.

When I was in the fourth grade my family moved from Chicago to North Hollywood, California. Dad suffered from lung congestion as long as we were in Chicago, and after a stay in the hospital and after smoking for thirty-two years he stopped cold and never smoked again. When he went out to visit Aunt Gerry and Uncle Bill, who had opened a linoleum store on Santa Monica Boulevard in Los Angeles, Dad found a job in a desk factory and stayed. Mother was left to sell the house, pack the furniture and move the family. She would have made all these decisions anyhow, but she complained bitterly about a man who would make her do it.

Dad had meanwhile bought a 1949 black Chevrolet, which helped convince us that we were going to Hollywood and be rich. We moved into a small house—too small for six people—on Riverton Avenue at the unfinished edge of a development where there were vacant lots to play in and a dead-end street still to be paved. Mother took a job doing photostat copying in an insurance company as soon as we arrived, and when Dad refused to go into debt to add on to the house, she said she would pay for it herself.

Our lives had shifted—without missing a mass—from St. Christina's church and school in Chicago to St. Patrick's church and school three blocks from our house in North Hollywood. I was an altar boy as soon as I was old enough in the fifth grade. We were chosen according to grades and behavior, but it also had something to do with personality and looks—a popularity contest as much as anything. I liked being singled out as special, being seen and recognized at the services, being part of the processions. There was a nice feeling of community, of belonging to something through the church—also we couldn't afford any kind of social activities except for those offered by the church. It was the only touch of elegance in our lives.

The assistant pastor would sometimes take the altar boys up to St. John's seminary for swimming and a picnic. I was a favorite of his—he called me "King David." Mother Anthony, the sister superior at the school, also called me that. She gave me a book about the biblical King David—with a picture in it of Michelangelo's sculpture of David—because she said reading about him might help me to control my temper.

While the church helped to satisfy our need to belong, the truth was the church offered no help at all with the real problems in our lives. This began with the church's unrealistic teachings about sex. You received your first communion at age six because that was when you were supposed to know right from wrong, to recognize a mortal sin when you saw one. I'll never forget the day because I scorched a new white silk tie trying to iron out a wrinkle in it and my parents made me feel like a criminal the whole day.

Even in grade school the priests would come by to give us lectures on morality. Thinking back on it, they seemed almost coy in their talks. They never spoke about sexual intercourse because that was forbidden, it was unthinkable that any of us would even consider it before marriage. I never heard them use the word heterosexual, much less homosexual. Boys and girls were trusted together through the eighth grade in the Catholic schools, then they were separated, with teachers of their own sex in high school.

Being one of the most popular boys, I was paired off with the prettiest girl. We were an attractive couple, and the nuns would often single us out for special favors. At parties she and I would get into some heavy petting and I would feel her breasts and, a few times, even indulge in French kissing, which of course was strictly forbidden. It provided an "occasion for sin" and it was "being intimate"—something reserved for marriage only.

I had special feelings for my buddies in grade school, but the only way this ever came out was in wrestling on the playground or jostling around a swimming pool. It may sound incredible, but I had never heard of masturbation when I first tried it. I was in the fifth grade and woke up one night with an erection protruding through my pajamas. It felt good rubbing against the cool sheets. For a long time that was the way I masturbated until I discovered it felt even better to use my hands.

One afternoon a school buddy and I were up in the top of a tree in our front yard, and he was telling me that "jerking off" was what priests were trying to say when they talked about "touching yourself in an impure way." Even so it took me a long time to make the connection. I never fantasized about boys or girls when I masturbated; the act itself was satisfying without images. None of my buddies ever mentioned to each other that they masturbated and that word was never pronounced by the priests. Instead they talked about "abusing yourself," about "impure thoughts."

This "sin" was about the only one I was capable of committing as a child. I always prayed for a wet dream, because that was not a conscious act and I didn't have to include it in my confession. Also, as long as I didn't use my hands I felt I was exempt. "Bless me, Father, I have sinned" were the words I had to say nearly every Saturday, but I would always bring in some other lesser misdeeds—"I sassed my folks three times"—so that my mortal sins wouldn't sound so bad on their own.

Sometimes the priest would say: "Well, you've got to try to be stronger, to be more resolved in your faith. You've got to try to be a better young man." Usually he would say nothing except to give a penance of Hail Marys and Our Fathers or—during Lent—the Stations of the Cross, which was the worst punishment of all. Not only did the Stations take a long time, but as you were doing them you kept seeing Jesus up there suffering because you had touched yourself in an impure way. In order to be forgiven you had to have a "firm purpose of amendment" and repeat the words, "I firmly resolve with the help of Thy grace . . ." I would say the words but I also knew I would do it again. I was overcome by guilt but my natural feelings always won out. Sexual arousal came very naturally to me. I liked the way it felt. But each time I had to live once more with the conflict over having promised never to do it again. The church, it seems to me, preyed on such natural conflict, and taught us to believe not through love and understanding but through fear and intimidation.

One Saturday I had to confess to a priest that I knew, which was worse because outside the confessional I had to live with his eyes following me, knowing what sins I had committed. I told him I had touched myself in "an impure way"—and at a time that was after my last confession and before receiving communion the next day. (The worst sin of all was to receive communion while in a state of mortal sin.) The priest was a balding, overweight man whose sermons were usually spent begging for more money for the church. He was very temperamental and shouted at me through the little window: "How dare you so totally abuse the laws of the church!" He ordered me to say the entire rosary and to stay silent in my room for the rest of that day and night. This particular Saturday we had people coming for dinner, and I couldn't talk to them, not even to explain why I was sitting in my room. In fact I was honestly frightened that I would be struck dead if I broke the penance, and convinced that I would suffer eternal damnation in hell as the priest had said I would.

I may be shaking my head about some of this as I recall it now, but these were genuinely terrifying experiences to me as a child. I learned a lot about fear and guilt through the church, and very little about compassion and love.

When I was in the eighth grade a member of the Claretian Order spoke at our school about the order's junior seminary, a boarding school preparing students for the priesthood. After a weekend visit to the seminary I decided to go there. I liked being the only one in my class who elected to go to the seminary. My guilt feelings about masturbation must also have entered into the decision, but I know—and my brothers and sister knew—the real reason was that I wanted to get away from home.

To me the seminary campus—called "Claretville"—on Dominguez Hill just ten miles south of downtown Los Angeles, seemed a well-ordered all-male paradise compared to the bickering I left behind at home. The campus included several acres of neatly-trimmed lawns sloping down from the main seminary buildings. The older seminarians lived in an adobe house built in 1825 as the seat of the Dominguez family's 75,000-acre Rancho San Pedro. There was a large formal rose garden in front of the old house, and surrounding the campus were wide green pastures where the Claretians raised and slaughtered beef cattle for their own use and for another seminary on the former Gillette estate in Malibu Canyon. Even into the 1960s there were miles and miles of open farmland stretching out from Dominguez Hill.

When I arrived there in the summer of 1956 the seminary was at the peak of its development with nearly 150 students in the junior—or minor—seminary alone. Ours was the first class to move into a new $300,000 building of modern poured concrete with terrazzo floors and huge wooden beams in the chapel. An expensive bell had been imported for the tower over the new chapel. In the courtyards between the buildings there was always a thick perfume from the neat rows of ligustrum and miniature gardenia bushes.

For many months I was very happy at the seminary. I even loved the strict routine—the outward sense of order eased my guilt, helped me forget the inner confusions about sex. At that time this had little to do with my being attracted to my own sex—I wasn't even aware that kind of sex was possible. It was simply my occasional indulgence in masturbation that bothered me—I enjoyed it; the church said it was evil.

Our days at the seminary began before dawn and we lived by rigid schedules, every minute accounted for. We slept in common dormitory rooms of about fifty beds each. We dressed in khaki military uniforms during the week and blue suits on Sundays. We marched—eyes straight ahead—to and from all classes, study halls and meals. We lived under a code of behavior spelled out in a little gray handbook called *The Mirror* and in solemn weekly lectures on morality given by the head prefect. We were not allowed to run, laugh or shout. Silence was enforced in the refectory, the lavatory and especially in the dormitory.

According to *The Mirror:* "The Claretian postulant shall ardently love and cultivate the beautiful lily of purity with the greatest care; thus, he will please his Heavenly Mother. Let him respect and even revere himself as a living temple of the Holy Spirit; thus, he will shun impure and dangerous imaginations as if they were flames from hell; will keep perfect modesty, especially in public; will flee particular friendships; and will never be idle . . . if any one should hear any word offensive to holy purity, notice any indecent action, or that someone is the object of too much familiarity on the part of any of his companions, the entire affair should be manifested to Father Prefect as soon as possible."

Physical contact was specifically forbidden and we were often lectured on keeping "modesty of the eyes." This meant that we could not look at each other. We never saw each other naked. The showers were inside stalls with doors, and we had to go in and out of them fully clothed. During recreation periods we were not allowed to lie back on the grass or around the swimming pool, presumably because this was a suggestive pose that might provide an "occasion for sin."

Even with every kind of sex forbidden, the brothers and priests were still visibly concerned about appearances and masculine manners. The best student in the grade ahead of mine was also one of the most serious and devout postulants, but he was never allowed to become a novitiate. The reason had to be his effeminate manners. His devotion was such that he eventually went to Europe, where he was able to join another order and become a priest.

In spite of the rules it seemed that everybody was paired off with a special friend. I was separated from most of my own class because I had made the varsity athletic teams even as a freshman. I never felt I had a best friend, but I did have two special relationships—one with a boy who was by far the best athlete in the school, the other with Father Ernest Hyman, the head prefect.

The athlete was two years older and a captain of the basketball team. He had blond hair, blue eyes, sharp features and stood six feet three. He moved with a real swagger. He wore taps on his shoes and kept his pants just a bit lower on his hips than the rest of us. We were like the two friends in *A Separate Peace* except that our competition was more evenly-matched. If we were on opposite teams in a basketball game it became a vicious struggle between the two of us. We competed so hard we would fight over the least infraction, and Father Hyman and the other students would often have to pull us apart. And yet, somewhere within all this outward violence there was a deep feeling between us. I wanted a sweater with a letter and captain's star just like his. If there was a movie we maneuvered so that we could sit next to each other. If we had to move the irrigation sprinklers in the pastures I would get myself assigned to his crew. In the refectory I always sat at his table, even though we weren't allowed to speak. When one of the brothers would pronounce the Latin phrase breaking the silence, we would cheer and talk together. When we took our summer vacations at the retreat in Malibu Canyon he and I were always in the same group swimming or hiking. I didn't recognize this as a sexual attraction then, but what I felt for him certainly was sexual. I knew the word homosexual, but I had no idea how it was acted out. I was also sure that I was not one of the "queers" and "fags" my brother and his buddies talked about beating up down at Coffee Dan's in Hollywood. When I masturbated I didn't think of my friend because I didn't think sex with him was possible. I just did everything I could to be close to him. When we would line up for showers, for example, I saw to it that I was in the stall next to him so that I could see his body reflected in the water on the floor under the partition between us.

The most lasting relationship I formed at the seminary was with Father Hyman. Even in that religious atmosphere athletics still reigned supreme. Father Hyman had been an outstanding athlete in college, so he naturally took a rather special interest in me. He named me an assistant infirmarian, a job that carried with it all sorts of privileges—I could leave study hall and chapel early, I could stay up after lights out. It was my first real taste of the privileges that go with being a good athlete in our society.

Although Father Hyman was a strict authoritarian he also responded to me with a kind of warmth and affection I had never felt from my father, and I responded to him. After he had an operation on his knee and his leg was in a cast he could not bend down to take off his socks. A few times after lights out I went to his room—which was off limits to everyone else—and although in a way it was humiliating to bend down and take off another man's socks and wash his smelly feet I did it. I felt very close to Father Hyman at these times. I felt I was really helping him.

When I went to Father Hyman to tell him I wanted to leave the seminary, it was the most difficult thing I had ever done. I had pleased him as an athlete; most of my studying had been to get an A in his religion courses. I felt I was letting him down, and he told me I was making the wrong decision, urging me to stay through the next summer. After eighteen months, though, I'd had enough of the life.

Ironically I think it was Father Hyman's encouraging me as an athlete that caused me to leave the seminary. Freedom to me at that time meant being able to join in competitive team sports with a band, cheerleaders and crowds behind me. Athletics at the seminary were mainly for recreation. We played only a few games away from our campus, and the only football was touch football. Even so, Father Hyman spent hours teaching me how to play the game. He was the one who first taught me how to punt and place kick, which I did very well in high school and in college and which also helped me to get my first position on a professional team, the San Francisco Forty-Niners.

One year when I was playing with the Forty-Niners I helped get tickets for Father Hyman and the entire seminary when we played Los Angeles. They sat as a group, and when I wasn't playing I could hear them cheering, "We want Kopay . . ." I took a lot of razzing from my teammates over that. Later I was to learn that many of my fellow seminarians were also homosexual and that they too had broken away from the church's strictures on sex and particular friendships.

My own break with the church coincided with my later awareness of my natural preference for sex with other men. The church's stand on homosexuality was unequivocal—and was restated in January 1976, by Pope Paul VI. While my awareness of this gap in the church's sensibility helped make me aware of other doctrines I disagreed with, mine was finally an uncomplicated decision. The church couldn't accept me in my natural state so I could no longer accept the church.

Joe Willie Namath, like many others, has also said the reason he left the Catholic church had to do with the church's attitudes on sex. In his book *I Can't Wait Until Tomorrow . . . 'Cause I Get Better Looking Every Day* Namath says: "But I stopped going to church a few years ago when a priest told me that I had to confess each time I'd been with a woman.

" 'Why?' I said.

" 'Because it's a sin,' he said.

"I don't think that's wrong. I really don't. I think if it's a beautiful thing and it makes two people happy, it's not wrong. Of course, the priest didn't agree with me at all. So I stopped going to church. I wasn't going to go to confession and lie, and I wasn't going to confess something I didn't feel was a sin. I wasn't going to be a hypocrite."

I feel the same way about having sex with men.

III

Eight

WHY I played football is a question as difficult for me to answer as why I am homosexual. I'm sure, though, that the origins of both are somewhere back there in the culture that produced me and in the special chemistry of my own body.

"It is the last private part of me," I said to Young as he kept pressing me to talk about the sport that had been the focus of my life. I have struggled to define the reasons why I might have dedicated myself to football with such intensity. In the articles and books I've read on the subject it seems to me that the writers are too quick to oversimplify it on the one hand and too quick to overcomplicate it on the other. To me football was never just a game. But then, neither was it ever just a job, a means of earning more money than I could elsewhere. I never thought of it as a "natural religion" as Michael Novak has called it. For almost twenty years football was life itself to me.

One of my former teammates, Rick Redman, says that you get into the sport with almost casual innocence. Somebody tells you that you're big and you ought to play football. You do well in high school, get a scholarship to college and pretty soon you're trying to get into the pros. Redman—all-American at the University of Washington in 1962 and 1963 and all-pro during his years with the San Diego Chargers—also says, "You're so young when you start. Anybody who is any good at this game started when he was too young to know what he was doing." Redman wasn't the stereotypical poor boy rising out of the ghetto through athletics, he was born to a wealthy family. But, he says, "I also liked the strokes I got from playing football."

I came into football by a process of elimination. Baseball was the big sport when I was a kid and that was the game I first wanted to play. But I suffered the humiliation of being told in high school that I wasn't good enough to make the team. The same went for basketball—I did earn a letter in that sport but I was never better than ninth man on the team. Track was my most difficult sport. I didn't enjoy it but I knew I had to endure it if I were ever going to star in football, and I managed to become the only three-letter student in the school at that time.

Between the ages of twelve and fourteen I grew into a six-foot, 175-pound giant of a boy. I also developed a painful inflammation of the knees known as Osgood-Schlatter's disease—the pain in my knees was so excruciating at times that I would fall on the floor when I bent over to adjust the television set, or to kneel in church. At the seminary there was no padding on the kneelers and for me this meant the prayers were always accompanied by physical pain.

From the beginning my involvement in sports was a struggle to overcome pain. Even as a child I knew I had to endure the constant pain in my knees if I were going to play football, and I felt I had to play football because that was the only way I could enjoy everything that went with being a star athlete.

The doctors had told me not to play ball with the other kids or to join in organized athletics at school, and my mother told this to the principal, who also tried to keep me from playing. I was only finally allowed to play after I won a long game of deception in which I convinced the principal that my mother and the doctors had said it was all right.

Maybe because of this early affliction, I was determined to find a sport where I could show people I was a normal, strong and healthy boy. Only recently I learned that the English word "agony" comes from the Greek word for athletics. That makes sense to me.

My parents never encouraged my interest in athletics; in fact they did everything to keep me from playing on my weak knees. My father said it was stupid of me to go on playing when the doctors had warned that I might end up in full leg casts. My mother was constantly worried that I would get hurt. My dad had never had the time to play any kind of sport and so he was never able to teach me any of them. He had never even thrown a baseball until a doctor prescribed it for treatment of bursitis when he was in his late fifties. I was amused—and proud too—to see him struggling to learn how to pitch at that age.

But if my parents were uninterested at first, they were later to seize on football as the great passion of their lives, offering as it did the one bit of recognition that lifted them out of their humdrum struggle to provide for the family. Until football the major diversion in our family had been a Sunday afternoon drive in the car. At the high school football games, which also were cheap, they could see Tony and myself out there in the spotlight with the whole community cheering us on. Almost every week the local paper, *The Valley Green Sheet*, would arrive with our names in it and sometimes a picture of us in a game.

My younger brother Gary says with some bitterness now that our parents deserved the suffering they brought on themselves after I spoke out on homosexuality. "It's because they made so much of that football thing," he says. Gary's wife recalls the time my mother referred to "my two sons," meaning the two who had played football.

Nine

ONE can only begin to understand the parents' shock over Kopay's homosexuality when one considers how deeply the mythology of masculinity is embodied in the sport of football. Kopay's parents accepted the myth as gospel. When he spoke out about his homosexuality, they took it to be a flagrant refutation of all they, and their neighbors, had admired in him.

Anthropologist William Arenes has written in *Natural History* that the football uniform itself "is not an expression but an exaggeration of maleness . . . The donning of the required items results in an enlarged head and shoulders and a narrowed waist, with the lower torso poured into skintight pants."

As in no other area of our society—except cloistered monasteries—females are generally excluded not only from playing the sport but from any involvement with the players prior to a game. As Kopay says, "If a boy performs badly during practice in high school, coaches are likely to harangue him about 'spending too much time with the girls.' Professional coaches say one reason they locate their training camps outside of the big cities is so the players can't get to the women. But many of the players develop friends and sex partners in these small towns where the training camps are. Still the coaches make a habit of not announcing nights off until the last minute. I remember that there were some college coaches who would even forbid their players to marry and many others openly discouraged it.

"From grade school on," Kopay says, "the curse words on the football field are about behaving like a girl. If you don't run fast enough or block or tackle hard enough you're a pussy, a cunt, a sissy." And Jim Bouton in *Ball Four* tells about his teammates, grown men in the major leagues, taunting each other with "Hey, sweetheart. Where's your purse, you big pussy?" And, "He'd lisp at me when I was going in to pitch. 'Is she going out and try it again today? Is she really going to try today?' "

Homosexuality in this setting is considered such a taboo the coaches and players not only feel free but obligated to joke about it. To be homosexual is to be effeminate, like a girl. "Cocksucker" becomes the ultimate insult. On one level they would insist on the complete absence of homosexuality among them. On another they are confirming its presence—in their minds, at least—by the endless banter and jokes about it. Billy Clyde Puckett, the fictional running back and narrator of *Semi-Tough*, uses the word "fag" twenty-two times in Dan Jenkins' short novel. David Kopay's story raises the question not how could he emerge from this super-masculine society as a homosexual, but how could any man come through it as purely heterosexual after spending so much time idealizing and worshipping the male body while denigrating and ridiculing the female.

Football surely represents one of the most rigid subcultures in America. In few other areas will young men be found willing and anxious to obey commands no matter how unreasonable they are. The coach is not only dictator and king but God (or a direct conduit to Him) as well. To question the coach in high school is to violate the first rule of the sport: obedience. To question the coach in college or professional football is to invite expulsion and fines. It is no coincidence that many of the more successful players and coaches in football are products of authoritarian Catholic backgrounds—as in Kopay.

Of all the team sports, football would also seem to be one of the most representative of the American character. A number of authorities are used to help define the game in *The First Fifty Years, The Story of the National Football League*, a book prepared by the creative staff of National Football League Properties, Inc.:

Konrad Lorenz in *On Aggression*—"The main function of sport today lies in the cathartic discharge of the aggressive urge." Vince Lombardi—"I think the nature of man is to be aggressive and football is a violent game. But I think the very violence is one of the great things about the game because a man has to learn control. He is going to go in and knock somebody's block off, and yet he must keep a rein on it." Wayne Walker, linebacker with the Detroit Lions— "Anybody who says this game is beastly, brutal and nasty, he's right." Paul Brown, coach of the Cincinnati Bengals—"I've known women who thought football was worthless and brutal. But they just don't understand the sport and they don't understand the nature of the male." Larry Wilson, safety on the St. Louis Cardinals—"This is one way for people to release their aggressions. I see them coming out of the stands, they are wringing wet with sweat, they are mad, they have played a football game and they look as beat up as the football players on the field." John Niland, tackle with the Dallas Cowboys— "Let's face it, most of the people in our society enjoy watching one guy knock down another one."

Some parents and sociologists recently were hopeful that football would be replaced by the safer sport of soccer. This has not happened; the explanations may lie within the American character.

Americans shared in the pastime of kicking around an odd-shaped ball that was the antecedent of European football or soccer. One historian cities evidence of such games in this country as early as 1609. The frontiersmen were known to take time out from drinking and gambling to kick around a blown-up pig's bladder. However the sport as it evolved in Europe was a toe dance compared to its counterpart in America. The "bloody Monday" games—ostensibly the same sport being played at Eton—were banned at Harvard in 1860 and at Yale in 1858.

American football is specifically derived from an offshoot of no-hands football in England. It was at a game in 1823 at the Rugby School when William Webb Ellis—according to a memorial tablet there—"with a fine disregard of the rules of football, as played in his time, first took the ball in his arms and ran with it."

Although the rules for soccer and rugby had both been formalized by that time, the first official "game" in this country in 1874 between Harvard and the McGill rugby team of Canada was peculiarly American. The McGill players may have thought they were introducing a new sport, but the Americans merely took some of the new rules and incorporated them into the game they were already playing. It has remained a sport played here as it is in no other country except Canada. "A love of football is one of the few interests we share with few outside our borders," says anthropologist Arenes, "but with almost everyone within them."

"There were few real choices later in my life," David Kopay says. "I had early decided on football as the way I would fit in and express myself in this society. I gave little or no thought to what I would do after I could no longer play football. The absolute physical expense of the sport was sufficient in itself. It also provided a convenient way for me—and who can say how many of my teammates?—to camouflage my true sexual feelings for other men."

Similarly, Bill Tilden, in Frank Deford's biography of him, is quoted as telling his court-appointed psychiatrist: "Sex has never been important in my life; I have had an outlet through athletics."

"I know from my experience that football is a real outlet for repressed sexual energy," Kopay says. "And to the extent that there's no other outlet—except in irrational violence toward innocent people—I think it's a healthy thing for the players and for the fans.

"The whole language of football is involved in sexual allusions. We were told to go out and 'fuck those guys'; to take that ball and 'stick it up their asses' or 'down their throats.' The coaches would yell, 'knock their dicks off,' or more often than that, 'knock their jocks off.' They'd say, 'Go out there and give it all you've got, a hundred and ten per cent, shoot your wad.' You controlled their line and 'knocked 'em into submission.

"Over the years I've seen many a coach get emotionally aroused while he was diagramming a particular play into an imaginary hole on the blackboard. His face red, his voice rising, he would show the ball carrier how he wanted him to 'stick it in the hole.' "

The sexual allusions help explain a player's passionate commitment to the game, as well as his difficulty in talking about it afterward.

Ten

FROM my first days in grade school I saw that the boys who were most popular with other students and most respected by the teachers were the best athletes. This was true even at the seminary. Naturally I wanted to be not just one of them, but the best of them.

Also, I was still chasing after my brother Tony. He was already a member of the high school athletic teams. He had a car. And he was more handsome—with finer features, a lighter body. Tony was a member of the coaches' inner circle, laughing and joking as if he were one of them.

When I got to Notre Dame High School from the seminary, one of my classmates was John Becker, a grade school buddy who was the first boy I was ever consciously attracted to sexually. It took years before I recognized it as that, but now I see a pattern with the friend at the seminary, with John in grade and high school and later with a fraternity brother in college.

I would imagine how they looked naked, or think sometimes about holding them—or, more often, about being held by them. With Becker, it was the same as with the others. In the absence of real physical love we communicated through competition—especially the competition of sports. As the seasons changed we played the different sports with equal spirit. If he was captain of one team, I would be the captain of another. We even competed for grades.

There was constant tension in the games I played. How much of this was sexual, I can't say for sure. I do know that the one I ended up fighting with the most—over the slightest difference about a call or a score—was John Becker, the one I was most attracted to.

This idea of competition as an expression of sexual feeling may be difficult for anyone to understand who has not been as committed to athletics as I have been. In an article published in the Sunday, May 21, 1972 *Washington Star*, George Sauer, then twenty-eight and just resigned as an all-pro wide receiver with the New York Jets, wrote: "The literal meaning of the word competition is to seek together, to strive together. The implication is that while opponents are set against each other, they are still doing something together with a common purpose . . . If competition is so deeply significant, it may be because it can bring opponents close, spiritually as well as physically, each providing the other with a challenge that will force them to call on all their reserves of skill and perseverance to seek beyond previous limits." Sauer also quoted from the scene in D. H. Lawrence's *Women in Love* in which two male friends respond to the sexual tension in their relationship by taking off their clothes and wrestling in naked embrace: "They became accustomed to each other, to each other's rhythm. They got a kind of mutual physical understanding. And then they had a real struggle. They seemed to drive their white flesh deeper and deeper against each other, as if they would break into a oneness . . . rapturously, intent and mindless at last, two essential white figures working into a tighter, closer oneness of struggle . . ."

For many years this kind of struggle represented the only sexual outlet I had except for masturbation. Many people have described this feeling we had for each other in the game, but they're all terrified that it might also include physical love. Coach Lombardi was always talking about love, but he would say he didn't mean physical love, he meant love in the sense of respect and loyalty for your teammates. A defensive back for the Forty-Niners when I played with them, told how Coach Bear Bryant reacted to all this talk of love: "I don't like you and you don't like me. 'Cause liking leads to lovin' and lovin' leads to fuckin' and don't you fuck the Bear."

I wonder now, why the coaches—or anybody else—are so

afraid of physical love with another man. Their fear of it only makes it more a monster—inside and outside their heads—than it really is. This fear of physical love kept me from a healthy, happy life for a long time. It's also the reason, I think, that few real friendships develop among football players. On the field we can get away with all kinds of physical affection men wouldn't risk showing anywhere else. We aren't ashamed to reach out and hug our teammates. After a touchdown you will see men embracing on the field like heterosexual lovers in the movies. We were able to hold hands in the huddle and to pat each other on the ass if we felt like it. I think these are healthy expressions of affection. What is unhealthy, I think, is that we are so afraid of expressing ourselves in the same way anywhere outside of the stadium, out of uniform.

Frankly I don't think all this ass-patting is necessarily an overt show of homosexuality. I do think that the fear of physical love that kept me and numerous teammates from developing deeper relationships reflects a serious confusion about homosexuality. The worst "fag haters" I knew in high school, college and in professional football were also the ones who seemed most confused about their own sexuality.

There was, for example, one coach in high school I would have done anything to please. He was violently temperamental and not very attractive physically—balding, overweight, pockmarked face. But his command over me and the other young athletes was almost absolute.

Coach Tim Dillingham [fictional name], was one of the few lay teachers at Notre Dame High School—a twenty-acre landscaped campus with low adobe-style buildings that is run by the Brothers of the Holy Cross. The brothers would never socialize with students after class as Dillingham would. In those days when the fashion was to "cut" somebody with disparaging remarks, this coach was the only teacher who dared engage in this kind of banter with students. He even joked about sex.

Like many other coaches, Dillingham used sexual slurs—
"fag," "queer," "sissy," "pussy"—to motivate (or intimidate)
his young athletes. The fear of being a "chickenshit" in the
coach's eyes was enough to keep us going long after we felt we
would drop.

I don't think it has to be this way. It is degrading to the
human spirit and to the dignity of sports. I think a coach
teaching love and loyalty can get his players to perform just
as well, if not better. One coach's sermons on "only the strong
survive" became a joke in high school after one of our
strongest teammates—who was later a heavyweight boxing
champion in the Navy—was found in the bushes, unconscious
from heat prostration.

Recently I called up my old high school buddy John
Becker—who is now head coach at the Valley Junior
College—to ask him why he thought we had worshipped Dillingham as we did. "Well," John said, "he knew more about
everything than anybody we knew at that time." I'd never
had any instruction in running—which is the key to almost
every sport, especially football. Dillingham showed me how
to crouch in a relaxed position, to keep my arms in and my
legs up under my body. Later these became reflex actions,
but I would never have known them if Dillingham had not
taken the time to teach me. I am one of several hundred
athletes who owe much of their success to the coaching we
got in high school from him.

Dillingham had been a star athlete himself in college. A
friend of mine once told me about another coach, also a star
athlete in college, who seemed to know more about sports
than anybody around. My friend—whose father had been a
professional football player—was a special favorite of the
coach. He had very strong legs, and the coach helped him
become a championship runner. Whenever we worked out,
he would lead the drills. If the coach said to run three 500s
or five 300s, he was out front running them himself and seeing to it that none of us slacked off.

58

During the summer between his sophomore and junior years my friend would meet with the coach for drills three and four times a week at a deserted park. Sometimes the coach would go home to dinner at my friend's house, where the coach was like a member of the family, staying up drinking and playing cards with the parents and often staying overnight.

There were whispers about "the scandal," but no one at the time really knew exactly what had happened. One day this coach didn't show up for the workouts in the park. Somebody said he had been suspended. Nobody could explain why. Many of his favorite students never saw him again.

Later, when I was becoming more aware of my own sexual preference, I asked my friend about what had happened to this coach. My friend said he had gone to bed "that night" and was asleep. He woke up to find the coach sitting there fondling him. His father had said to him, "If I had my way I'd see he was locked up." My friend told me, "He is a very sick man."

Of course at that time I couldn't tell my friend that I didn't see this as a sickness. What I now see as a sickness, more than the act itself, was the kind of repression that drove the coach to commit an act he knew would get him into serious trouble.

I also believe the fear of such a thing happening between myself and a student is exactly why I can't get a job as a coach right now. At least that would be the excuse offered if anybody privately asked the coaches and owners why they wouldn't hire me.

The fact is, most homosexuals I know are no more attracted to young boys than heterosexual men are to young girls. Whatever the sexual preference, though, most people take notice that a young boy is shaping into a handsome man or a fine athlete just as they do that a young girl is becoming a beautiful woman. And there is nothing new about this. The following is from Socrates: ". . . I confess that I was quite astonished at his beauty and stature; all the world seemed to be enamored of him; amazement and confusion reigned when he entered; and a troop of lovers followed him. That grown-up men like ourselves should have been affected in this way was not surprising, but I observed that there was the same feeling among the boys; all of them, down to the very least child, turned and looked at him, as if he had been a statue . . ."

But it's wrong to suppose that this kind of attention is going to lead to sexual overtures. "Dear Abby" advises parents troubled by someone in the family who is openly gay that this person is far less a threat than a married uncle who has suppressed his homosexuality but is always bouncing junior on his knee.

What people are really saying, when they say that homosexuals can't be trusted as coaches or teachers, is that homosexuals are somehow different from heterosexuals in being unable to control their sexual feelings in a professional public situation. My own career helps give the lie to this. I was a complete professional on the field and in the locker room. As a coach or teacher today I would no more make a pass at a young athlete I found attractive than I would have during my playing days at one of my teammates.

I guess this attitude that homosexuals are not to be trusted comes from the long years of silence, when the only time the subject was mentioned at all in public was in connection with the publicized rare occasions when an older man had molested a younger boy. The only homosexuals people heard about were the few who pushed themselves into the public eye by committing rape or molesting a minor. There are laws on the books—dealing equally with heterosexuals and homosexuals—to punish such acts, which are very different from what takes place between consenting adults in private.

It is a secondary point that I am not sexually attracted to young boys. The real point is that if somebody put me—or any other homosexual I know—in a room full of males I wanted to go to bed with I could and would control my feelings and carry out my professional duties.

My friend's coach was a type one often sees in the world of sports. Although a knowledgeable coach, he also was apparently a product of sexual repression—temperamental, unhappy, his anger expressing itself in sometimes brutal punishment of the young athletes under him. I myself had a coach in high school who literally ran us into a fence to see if we would obey him. In 105-degree heat he would allow no water breaks during three hours of practice. To me this kind of behavior represents something far more disturbing than a man who is dealing openly with his homosexuality.

My friend from grade school and high school, John Becker, is now in a position to hire me at the college where he's head coach. I asked him if he would consider it. "Absolutely," he said. But isn't he afraid of the problems this might cause? "I don't see any problems," he said. He talked about a course he's teaching in which the students learn about all kinds of sexual expression. He added that he believed a homosexual coach—having suffered repression himself—might be more sensitive in dealing with younger athletes. He wasn't at all worried about a coach getting involved with a student. "That would be between you and him," he said.

"You know, Dave," said John, who is now happily married, "I've got three gay friends and you're the only one who's never made a pass at me." I had to laugh. "Well, John," I said, "it's not because I never wanted to."

When I first started playing football the only thing that mattered to me was getting the ball and running with it. I didn't really understand the intricacies of the game. The point seemed to be either getting the ball away from somebody or catching it and making a first down or touchdown. I loved that wonderful free feeling, running down the field with the crowds cheering, and knowing that my parents were up there cheering too. I was tough and aggressive enough when I was running with the ball, when I was getting hit myself. But when it came to going after other guys, I was very frightened.

61

I overcame all that when I got to college but for a long time I knew you could get hurt making a tackle much easier than getting hit yourself. The power of your own momentum, when you're running toward somebody gives extra confidence and force.

I really wasn't a total football player in high school because I was mainly interested in the superficial glory of the game—the immediate rewards that went with a first down or a score. After the games Dad would come by and shake my hand. About all he ever said was, "Good game," but other people would tell me how he bragged about me to them. I especially remember the last game my senior year. We played Banning High School and they beat us something like 51-0, but it was also one of the best games I played that year. I was very excited afterwards. I carried the ball twenty-one times and rushed for 120 yards. I punted. I kicked off. I even got two interceptions. I was smiling as we left the field because I kept thinking—hey, I did my job. Dad was very excited too. He was behaving as if we won because I had such a good game myself.

After that game we realized that I did have a chance to get a scholarship for college. I made the all-Catholic conference team and the scholarship offers began to come in. College for me had never before been discussed. The money simply hadn't been there. Now I was able to get an alternate appointment to the Naval Academy, but I finally decided I would take a scholarship at Marquette—it was a Catholic college, it was near my mother's family in Chicago and my high school friend Mike Merkle was already there. But after that fall Marquette discontinued its football program. I could have kept my scholarship but I saw no reason to stay if I couldn't play ball. I then talked to the University of Colorado and was offered regular cash payments for pocket money, free clothes and a car if I would accept a scholarship. My brother Tony was already there when I went home for Christmas. He was now a member of the University of Washington's Rose Bowl team, and some of the players came by our house. They seemed small compared to the guys I would have played with at Marquette, and I kept thinking I could do that, I could be on a Rose Bowl team too.

Our whole family went to the game that New Year's Day, and although Tony didn't get to play we were still proud. He was part of the spectacle and so were we. Once again I wanted to be where my brother Tony was.

Eleven

COACH Jim Owens once told a group that he arrived in Seattle, took one look at Mount Rainier and knew he had come to stay. One is either captivated by the beauty of the place or leaves very quickly because of the wet weather.

It is a city with the clean, fresh feeling of a mountain lake town. On any of the several steep hills that make up Seattle, you are never out of sight of the water—of Lake Washington and Lake Union and the Puget Sound. Forming a spectacular backdrop to the city are the snow-covered Cascade Mountains in one direction, the Olympics in another and rising like some ancient monument to the south, Mount Rainier itself.

The main campus of the University of Washington is high enough to afford a view of all these mountains. The central mall is laid out with a direct view of Mount Rainier, as if in homage to it. Especially in springtime, the place is as colorful as any place in America. Because of the constant moisture there is a rich abundance of flowers. It is one location where a yard full of flowers can be described as riotous with color. Tree-sized rhododendrons with single blossoms as delicate and as large as rubrum lilies abound in purples and pinks, alongside bright orange and yellow azaleas. Mallards in their bright colors waddle around the lush green campus lawns and neighboring yards as confident as if they had paid tuition.

I took one look at the place in 1961 and knew I had found a home. I still think about going back. I arrived at the University of Washington in midyear but I was still given the VIP tour of the city by boat and plane, ending at the lodge beside Snoqualmie Falls with a breakfast banquet of fresh fruits, pancakes, bacon, sausage, eggs and biscuits and sweet rolls and fireweed honey.

I was offered none of the extra benefits I had been promised by other schools, but I was happy with my scholarship, with the beautiful city and the chance to play for a championship team.

In 1961 Coach Owens and the University of Washington football team were enjoying the peak of a long and successful history of championship seasons. Owens' teams had just won two successive Rose Bowl games, defeating the champion Big Ten teams from the east. His record had been topped only by one of the first coaches at the school, Gil Dobie, who left after nine undefeated seasons.

Football at Washington was almost as old as the university itself. The first game was played by a group of Ivy League veterans in 1889, which was also the year a fire swept through the downtown area, nearly leveling the heart of the city. The football games offered a rallying diversion, and from the beginning aroused unusually spirited support in the city where the last frontiersmen ran up against the sea—actually where they caught the boats going back and forth to the Alaskan frontiers. In 1920 more than $320,000 was raised in Seattle to build—in six months—the first major football stadium on the West Coast, and almost all of that money came from the sale of $50 and $100 season tickets. The new horseshoe stadium opened onto Lake Washington, where some of the fans docked their boats during the games. The snow-covered Cascades are straight behind the eastern goal and Mount Rainier is visible due south of the fifty-yard line. In 1950 a huge extra tier of seats with a high, unobstructed cover was built above the southern side, raising the seating capacity to 56,000.

There are no words to describe accurately the feeling of your first exposure to that stadium from inside. After anxious hours of tedious preparation the team is suited up and rumbling down the boardwalk through the narrow dark tunnel that leads from the locker room into the heart of the sunlit arena. The noise of sixty pairs of cleats clomping on the boards is almost deafening in itself, but above that is the sound of the band playing "Bow Down to Washington" and the crowds roaring as the team starts coming out.

As a nervous young sophomore I ran onto the field for my first regular season game. It was against Purdue. I was the starting halfback with a team that had just won two Rose Bowls in a row. I took my place to kick off. I glanced up at the awesome tiers of seats rising—as if straight overhead—to the height of a sixteen-story building (looming like some giant steelwork model of a prehistoric bird in flight), and wet my pants.

By coincidence my years at Washington were to parallel Coach Owens' last days of glory there. Owens—tall, lean and rugged—started there in 1957, two months before his thirtieth birthday. He had been an all-American at Oklahoma and came to Washington after serving as Bear Bryant's assistant coach both at Kentucky and Texas A&M.

Owens instilled a Spartan brand of training that is still talked about in Seattle—especially his "death march" in which he drilled his players back and forth from one end of the field to the other. One sportswriter said that the veterans who survived that march were "the core of the corps that in time wrung out two Rose Bowl champions. The last survivors of the 'death march' were among the 20 stalwart seniors who were the nucleus of the Rose Bowl champions of 1960 and 1961. They are gone. About 83 young men will turn out for the spring rituals Friday. Now—goes the rumor—is the time for Owens to start all over again and break 'em in right with another 'death march.' "

I was among the eighty-three reporting for practice that spring of 1961. We all accepted the rigid training as the way things had to be if we were going to make it to the Rose Bowl again for Coach Owens. Did anybody ever question Owens' strict approach to training? Question him? One of my teammates who asked not to be quoted answered that question with "man, you didn't even *speak* to Jim Owens. Do you understand that was like talking to God?" We half-seriously believed that Owens could have walked to work from his house on the other side of the lake.

But to a man we also relished the tough image of the team—as for example in a column titled "TV Horror Program" by Jim Murray in the October 31, 1963, *Los Angeles Times:* "I won't say Owens gets the toughest, hungriest football players in the West each year," Murray wrote, "but if they were in the Roman Colosseum the lions wouldn't come out. The worst injuries they fear year in and year out are bones in the throat. Not theirs, the other guys'! After every play, the other team always takes roll call. On goal-line stands, the Washington front line needs toothpicks after every play. They've got this one lineman named Redman who, I think, eats bear meat on the hoof. I am told that when he leans over the line of scrimmage he calls out to the enemy backs, 'If you're coming through here, would you mind putting a sprig of parsley behind your ear or an apple in your mouth? Aids the digestion.' The way Washington plays the game, the Catholic boys can't even scrimmage on Fridays. I fully expect USC to take a head count Saturday and if they come up one short, the captain will go over, tap Redman on the chest and say, 'OK, wise guy, we know you got Willie Brown in there. Now, cough him up.' "

The bedtime curfews during training and the regular season were strictly enforced and the players were required to live together in the Conibear Shellhouse—an airy shingle barn of a place built on stilts over the lake as a storage place for crew shells and other equipment. The mosquitos were fierce, there often was the smell of a nearby garbage fill, and the sleeping cots were uncomfortable. There was no problem with girls, one of my teammates told a Seattle reporter, "because we never get to see any of them."

67

Twelve

FOOTBALL was the only way I ever got to college and it was the only reason I stayed there. As for the academic side of college, I was allowed to take a reduced schedule because of my involvement in football. That meant that I wasn't ready for graduation when the rest of my class finished, and I completed the work for my degree in history in two semesters during the off-season after I started playing professional football.

In *The Joy of Sports* Michael Novak describes football as a "corporate game, a game of solidarity, an almost socialistic experience." This was certainly true for me. In college everything I did was focused on the team. The worst thing I could do was to "let the team down," and the fear of this kept me and the others driving toward that "hundred and ten per cent" the coaches were always yelling for.

Although at the time I felt I deserved my place, I now think I was moved into the starting lineup too soon after I arrived at Washington. Following our first practice sessions in the spring of 1961 I was on the first team that played in the May alumni game. That fall in the regular season game against Purdue I made the opening kickoff and did all the punting. This is how *The Seattle Times* described it: "A blossoming punter, Kopay was worried. One swallow does not a summer make. Nor one football game a punter. But footballs soaring off the ample toe of Dave Kopay provided astonished gazes among Purdue defenders and joyous murmurs in the throng of 55,000 witnesses to Washington's first game of the season. On four kicks, Kopay averaged almost 42 yards. One dropped dead on the Boilermaker 4-yard line—56 yards from scrimmage and almost 70 from where Kopay kicked it."

That story was prophetic. I had made my place on the team through my abilities as a punter and kickoff man, but after a bad kick during a game in midseason I lost my confidence and never managed to come back as a kicker. By the end of the season I wasn't even starting, and during spring practice the next year I was shifted on down from the first to the second to the third team. I sat on the bench during most of the 1962 season.

I think what had happened was that the coaches, attracted by my kicking ability, were led to give me a chance to prove myself in other areas. But the fact was that I just wasn't ready for the starting assignment they gave me. There was no way, though, that I would have admitted this to myself at the time. I liked being in the center of the field, kicking off to the roar of the crowds and punting in crucial moments. When they started shifting me downward, I couldn't admit that the players replacing me had more ability than I had and that I wasn't even developing the potential I did have. Since most of the running backs were black, I credited their success to "reverse discrimination." Of course it wasn't that, it was just that I needed an excuse for my own shortcomings.

Coach Chesty Walker, a father figure to the players as well as to Coach Owens, was especially popular with the black players. After a while I came to realize he was just a decent, understanding man, but at first I accused him of favoring the blacks over me. Even when I did this he stayed calm and understanding. He pointed out that the black players we had happened to be better runners, better qualified in other ways too. He said if I were going to play I would have to play hard to get where I wanted to be, that I should stop this feeling sorry for myself, stop blaming other people and start working to sharpen my own playing.

I came to feel a real love for Chesty Walker. He had responded to me and I wanted to please him. I would bust through on a run, break two or three tackles at the line of scrimmage and make ten or fifteen yards, then come back to the huddle hearing Chesty calling out, "Pick up your feet, David, keep running, keep 'em churning." I knew Chesty Walker cared, and I gave it all I had for an approving wink or pat from him. I did make a comeback and I think he was as happy as I was when I made it in professional football. We remained close friends until he died.

My brother Tony was an assistant coach that year, and although he and I fought like hell over his criticism of my performance in practice, when I would get really low and threaten to quit Tony would also encourage me to hang in.

During these rough times my mother contributed this poem:

> Life's battles don't always go
> To the strongest or fastest man;
> But sooner or later the man who wins
> Is the man who thinks he can.

I had earned a letter my sophomore year but I didn't play enough my junior year, so that at one point I was suiting up as the fifth-team defensive guard, and my senior year I walked around with the sweater of a one-year letterman even though by then I had made a comeback that caused the sports writers to describe me as a Horatio Alger.

Our teams of 1961 and 1962 didn't qualify for the Rose Bowl, but we did make it after the 1963 season. I played every game that year and by the time of the Rose Bowl my teammates had named me a permanent co-captain, an honor always connected to regular-season game performance.

The day after I was elected co-captain we were having a "shell" practice—helmets, T-shirts, shorts and shoes—just before the Rose Bowl game. A younger defensive back came up and hit me full speed in the side with his head, separating two ribs from the cartilage. It felt like somebody had jabbed a knife into me.

That night the pain was so intense I could hardly sit down. I could see all my fine dreams going down the drain. I was to start on both offense and defense, and there was no way a second string man could have replaced me. I knew I had to play because I was the only one who could do the job right. I could not let the team—or myself—down. Just before the game a doctor gave me a "block shot," an injection of novocaine or xylocaine that was supposed to block the feeling in my side, but this didn't stop the pain, the dull ache was still there.

By the time we were on the field, I was totally caught up in the excitement. Everyone I knew in the world was watching this game, and as co-captain I walked out to the center of the field to call the toss. When we won it I jumped two feet off the ground, feeling no pain.

This was one of the most rewarding parts of the game to me, my vital dependency on my teammates and theirs on me. It wasn't just that you'd get your own block knocked off if you didn't make the right moves, you could also get your teammates hurt. It was the most basic feeling of knowing you needed other people and knowing they needed you.

My membership in the Theta Chi fraternity was more or less an extension of the football experience. Nobody in my family had ever belonged to a fraternity and I didn't really know that much about it. But several of the other players belonged to this fraternity and I wanted to do what they were doing.

One night Ray Mansfield and Johnny O'Brien, members of Theta Chi, asked me to the house for dinner. Mansfield had started on the championship Rose Bowl team the year before, was all-American in college and is still the starting center on the Pittsburgh Steelers. He was square-jawed, thick-necked, tall and heavy, but with features more defined than most men's of that weight. He looked like he could wrestle a bear. He was one of the toughest members of a team known as one of the roughest in America. Off the field he was—and

71

remains—a gentle, considerate friend, as well as a family man with three children.

Johnny ("O'B") O'Brien was the class wild one, always getting penalized by the fraternity for some outrageous stunt—at a formal party or dance he would do a back flip off a table or a hook slide across the dance floor. I asked him why. "Look," O'B said, "in high school I was all-conference and all-state, a real star. But I got here to college and was just a little guy, another member of the team. This was how I kept in the spotlight." He meant that literally. Inevitably there would come a time at every function when O'B would take over the spotlight, hanging from a balcony or rafter, pants half-masted to his ankles.

To me the Theta Chi house seemed like a castle, and in fact it was on "Greek Row," a beautiful tree-lined street coming straight up the hill from the main gate to the university. But my joining it had little to do with a try for the elegance missed in my childhood. As an athlete in high school and college I never felt cheated because I didn't have money for a car or expensive clothes. I felt rich in praise and recognition, and for a while that seemed to be enough.

Mansfield had told me to get dressed up for this dinner at the fraternity house—it was a chapter meeting, the meal was served by pledges in white jackets. Everybody sang the fraternity song, then the president asked a member to pray— the Catholics always said the same thing; the Protestants made up the words as they went along. It was the very first time I had lived that close to Protestants.

I hadn't realized that I was being "rushed." I didn't know what that was. But after dinner the president said, "Well, we have Dave Kopay here and he's chosen to pledge Theta Chi." They all went wild cheering and applauding and slapping me on the back. And I loved it. For them it was as if they had won a game against the other fraternities—they all fought over athletes—but I had never looked any place besides John and Ray's house.

The next fall when I helped in the recruitment of other athletes, Rick Redman was the real "nugget"—a high school all-American football player, handsome, good student, wealthy family. The perfect pledge. In fact looks had a lot to do with who was chosen during rush, although we'd never say outright that we thought a certain guy was good-looking. We would call him "studly," and the ugly ones "squeezes" or "nipples" or "dings." After the rush parties we would meet to go over the roster. "Well, he really wasn't very studly, but he's a nice guy," somebody would say. "We've got enough nice guys." "Yeah, but he'd be good for the grade point average. We could put him at the back of the pictures so the women won't notice . . ."

Hell Week—or hazing—came during the spring. The pledges had to scrub all the floors, paint almost every wall in the house, wear "dingle bells" around their cocks and Kotex belts soaked in molasses without taking them off the whole week. Some nights the cook would make extra spaghetti and we would get into food fights at dinner—splattering the walls the pledges had just cleaned so they would have to clean them again.

The "line-ups" at all hours of the night were sometimes cruel exercises in physical endurance, usually staged in the hot, stuffy basement recreation room. Pledges were ordered to jump up and down to make their dingle bells ring, were called by their pledge names—"dog shit," "puberty breath," "tiny cock," "shit mouth." Winners of the biggest cock contests in years past were known as "Lord Chesterfield."

Often the older brothers would berate the pledges, saying they hadn't done anything worth a shit so they deserved so many whacks with a paddle. If, for example, there was some guy I didn't like, I'd say, "Bend over, I'm gonna give you five." And he had to say, "Thank you, Honorable Brother Kopay."

The pledges went through an exhausting routine of calisthenics—running in place, upsy-downsies, then they'd be broken down into relay teams for races, running with their mouths full of bitter alum water until a bucket had been filled, or picking up an olive off a block of ice with the crack of their ass and running with it. The loser had to eat the olive.

Sometimes the pledges would be allowed to take off their molasses-soaked Kotex belts if a bad rash broke out; they could also put band-aids over their nipples when the sackcloth uniforms had rubbed them raw.

I was on the receiving end of the paddles during my initiation into the Big We Club after I had earned a letter playing football my sophomore year. It was assumed all lettermen would join the Big W Club, which had no meetings, no functions except the initiation dinner at one of the bigger fraternity houses. There were rumors about how rough the initiation was. At the Theta Chi house I had managed to get around the paddling. Sometimes a brother with a particular grudge would get an athlete to paddle somebody who was named for punishment. Or there would be an auction for the privilege of paddling somebody who wasn't liked.

Here I had been a hot-shot athlete from the time I arrived and now I was about to get mine. Only a few of the athletes in my class had earned letters—Rick Sortun, who later played six years with the St. Louis Cardinals, and Jake Kupp, who was captain of the New Orleans Saints for several years. Here were some of the toughest guys on campus walking up to the Big W initiation full of nervous apprehension about what was to happen.

After an ordinary sit-down fraternity dinner the president announced that the initiation would be carried out in the living room. I was feeling a chill sickness in my stomach as I watched them form chairs and couches—backs outward—into a tight circle. We lined up behind them and waited. I whispered to my buddies that we should get the hell out while there was time. But there was no way to leave, even though none of this made any sense except that it was what everybody else was doing. They told us to take off our sweaters, take everything out of our pockets. Anybody wearing double shorts or padding would get hit twice as much. Paddles were passed out to the sixty members, those with the most letters having the honor of going first. Each member was allowed one swat for every letter earned.

It got to be incredibly brutal, and it seemed that the ones you knew best were the ones who beat you the hardest. There were some cracks about this one or that one somebody didn't like, but generally they kept their remarks on a joking level as they were beating us—they could get away with the vicious paddling as part of the initiation but they would have to answer for their words outside.

The outline of my shorts had been beaten into my skin and I felt like I was on fire as I made my way back to the fraternity house, went upstairs to the head, pulled my pants down and looked in the mirror. My ass was black and blue, covered with blood blisters. It was two full weeks before I could sit down without a painful reminder of the Big W Club initiation.

I thought I was nuts to have done something like that, yet the next year—and the next—I was there to get my turn behind the paddle. Of course the ones I was paddling were not the ones who had paddled me. But it seemed to indicate your status if you took part, hit hard and let them know you could do it.

My brother Tony had transferred to Washington from a junior college, and since most pledges are brought in as freshmen he was too late to join a fraternity. But he was popular and often invited to the parties, at one of which I caused a fight that almost cost him an eye. I had decided to play Mister Tough with some guys there we thought were party crashers. Later I said one of them was talking "trash" with one of our girls, which I'm sure I made up to justify what I did. I took a swing and missed one of them on the couch. Two of them grabbed me, ripped my shirt off and pinned me down on the floor. Mike Merkle got smashed in the head with a beer bottle. Tony and two of his friends rushed in from another room. One of them tattooed the face of one of the crashers with his Rose Bowl ring. Tony was wrestling with the one I started the fight with. He got him in a head lock on the floor, but the other guy had a hold on Tony's Rose Bowl watch. Tony was screaming that he would kill the guy if he didn't let go of the watch, but the guy got a hold on Tony's head and began gouging his eye before he was pulled off.

I, the hero of the night who hadn't landed a punch, joined in the buddy-buddy talk after the fight but for days after felt guilty. I knew Tony almost got his eye gouged out in a fight I had started to get attention, to make myself look tough in my buddies' eyes—and in my brother's eyes too.

That was my last fight—except on the football field, where I was known to square off and slug it out with anybody I thought had taken a cheap shot, regardless of how big and bad he was. I know I'd never have fought these same guys on the streets. Few things could make me feel that kind of anger off the football field. If I had any kind of aggression or anger to work out, the football field was the proper and acceptable place for it.

I had always known that with my size and my capacity for violence I could really hurt somebody. I don't think that capacity is any greater than the average office worker's, but I'm aware I have the strength to back it up. In a fight it would be all over unless the other guy killed me first. That is why I've developed a "look that could kill" that has sufficed as a convincing warning to people that I want to think I might kill them even though I've never tried.

Fights were common among my college teammates. For some these fights—and more important the talk before and after—were another way of fraternizing, a physical kind of communication among friends who couldn't verbalize or act out in any other acceptable way their real feelings. Others joined in because that's what they felt was expected of them in the spirit of fraternity, they didn't want to be left out, be considered chicken. The same went for talk—once it started it snowballed in its crudity and toughness. Somebody would start with some crack about women or fags—or about shit, a major preoccupation in locker room humor—and the topping game would be on. Dick Wetterauer, a college teammate and also an art student, says he lived two separate lives in college. "In the locker room I was the crudest of the crude," but with his girl friend and in the classrooms, he was sensitive and serious.

I know I didn't hate fags or women, and I didn't really enjoy all the crude talk—but I joined in. It was another way of not dealing with real feelings.

In the summer of 1963 the coach got jobs for me and two other players on an offshore oil rig out from Anchorage, Alaska. For college students, with its guaranteed overtime and all expenses paid up and back, it was a high-paying job. A powerful crew-boat with two big Cat-Nine diesel engines cut right across the waves taking us the seventy miles out to the rig, where the operation was drilling down to try to save another hole that the year before had blown up and now been set on fire to cut down on the water pollution. The fire was consuming enough oil and gas each day to heat the city of Anchorage for a whole year. It was June by then but it was biting cold and pouring rain when we made the treacherous leap from the crew-boat onto the rig, an old destroyer with the ends lopped off and anchored at four corners.

There was no radio, no television, and we got into town only one night while we were there. Our one luxury was the elaborate food prepared by a French cook, an interesting fellow who'd work twelve hours a day, seven days a week, for six months so that he could live comfortably on the Riviera for the other six months. The rest of the twenty-eight men on the crew were rough and rugged, but I never heard any of them say anything derogatory about the cook, although everybody knew he was homosexual. He took especially good care of us three husky college football players. We were also an appreciative new audience for his stories, and once he invited one of my buddies into his cabin to look at some pictures of men he said he had had sex with.

I relished the cook's stories about the places he had been, but I also would like to have seen the pictures my buddy described. I was afraid, though, to get too close to the cook, afraid that he and my friends might find out my own still very private desires.

My best friend in college was Ted Robinson [fictional name]. Ted was also Ray Mansfield's "little brother" and close friend in the fraternity. He had been a high school basketball player and in our one-on-one games he still competed with the seriousness of a true athlete. He was blond, had a long V-shaped face with a deep dimple in his chin. His shoulders were narrow and his upper body slender, but his hips and legs were those of a well-trained athlete. Later when he started to get a slight paunch I would kid him about getting out of shape.

We were both members of the fraternity basketball team and spent a good deal of time together practicing and working out. We were also both sun-worshippers and every chance we got in spring and summer we would be out studying or reading in the sun, usually off by ourselves at the beach or Green Lake, or sometimes just sitting on the rooftop sun deck of the fraternity house, a fine place from which to launch water balloons—also from which to shoot beavers through the windows of the next-door sororities. It was another shared experience of the brothers focusing their attention on the girls, while getting off on their own feelings of camaraderie.

Looking back I don't think Ted and I really ever talked about anything very seriously. We certainly never discussed our feelings, especially for each other. Mostly it would be about what we were going to wear to a party or which girls we were hustling that week.

Ted always wore one of my football jerseys at the Bowery

Brawl, Theta Chi's annual party usually held in some barn out in the country or at a warehouse in town. We had different kinds of dates for different functions—the sorority girls for more formal occasions, less "classy" girls for the Brawl and similar functions.

I also had a girl reserved just for sex. Occasionally I would feel guilty about this, I thought I was using her. Now I realize she was years ahead of me in her sexual liberation. If anything she was using me because sex was all she really wanted out of me. She had large firm breasts, with strikingly big nipples that pointed up when she was naked. She had already made it with my brother Tony and some others on the team, but I came to her absolutely inexperienced in sex. The first time I had an orgasm just in foreplay—and she was a good teacher. Her ass reminded me of Ted's—the fine muscles of an athlete. Sometimes we would go out for a beer, but I never took her on a real date. I would just call her up after I had been out drinking and she was always willing. One time after a recruiting speech a teammate pretended to be passed out on the next bed in a motel room so that he could watch us have sex. In the process he got so excited he fell out of bed and we had to finish off in the shower.

My room at the fraternity was in an old building, an annex to the main fraternity house, where I would sometimes take this girl. One night Ted managed to put a tape recorder under the bed. After I took her home I came back to find a group of fraternity brothers gathered about listening to the recording on the tape. I yelled at them to erase the tape and they pretended to do it, but they also knew that I didn't know how to work the machine. Long after that I discovered they were still playing that tape and laughing.

Beneath Ted's horseplay and all our silliness, of course, there were deeper feelings. Ted was somebody who seemed to respond to me with a special warmth, and that was something I had never known in a friend. It felt good just being with him.

We would drink a lot of beer in those days, which seemed to be the only way we could really get close to each other. One night, back from a round of drinking, we ended up in each other's arms on one of the beds on the fraternity's sleeping porch. We kept our clothes on, but I had an orgasm just from rubbing against Ted and holding him. Not long after that, when we were sleeping in the annex, we found ourselves on the bed in my room. We had taken our dates home and were just lying on the bed holding each other when somebody came up to the door. We panicked, jumped out of bed and yelled that we were just fooling around and getting ready for bed. At other times we would go down to one of the private study rooms to read or listen to music, and would end up first scuffling and then holding each other. Usually after we had been out drinking we would stop by the Hasty Tasty for breakfast, and a couple of times instead of going back to the fraternity house we stopped off at a motel. The next morning neither of us would talk about what we had done. "God, did we really stop by the Hasty Tasty last night, I don't remember a thing . . ."

Awkward as these experiences were, they did, I think, represent a real love, and a natural desire for sex, between us. What we didn't know was how to go about it. Homosexuality was something we had repressed so strongly we hadn't even considered the ways two men have sex—which, after all, aren't so different from the ways many heterosexual couples have sex, but that hadn't occurred to us.

Ted was always receptive to my caresses and often would encourage me with a word, a look or a gesture that I naturally understood. I always had an orgasm, I don't think he ever did. I suppose this was another way of telling himself that he wasn't really homosexual, that we weren't really doing what we were doing.

At first Ted liked me to simulate heterosexual intercourse with our clothes still on. Later we did get around to taking our clothes off before we "passed out" in bed together, especially when we went to a motel. I was ready to do more than just rubbing and holding him. I had had fantasies about oral sex for several years, but I always thought of it as something only a woman could do. I knew, though, that a real desire for it was in me too. After a while I was able to have oral sex with Ted, but he never could with me. What he liked most was helping me "get off," watching me have an orgasm. I suppose this was his way of saying it was my doing, not his. Not being the aggressor he wasn't responsible for what I did.

I think much of my attitude had to do with my acceptance of the traditional masculine and feminine roles in sex—the male, aggressive and on top; the female, passive and on the bottom, performing to give pleasure to the male. Most of us have come to accept now that our sexual responses aren't necessarily "manly" or "womanly," including those of heterosexuals. Today fewer and fewer straight couples stick rigidly to the traditional roles during sex. There is also no reason why homosexual couples should have to rely on the old strictly passive or aggressive roles—there is no reason why both partners—homosexual and heterosexual—shouldn't do what seems natural and feels good.

Just as I had been having fantasies in those days about how a woman felt while she was performing oral sex on a man, I also wondered about how she was feeling during regular intercourse—how I would feel, in a similar position, in anal intercourse with a man. It would be several years before I acted this out, and even though it had been somewhere in the back of my mind for a long time I never consciously admitted to such fantasies—I never even admitted to myself that it was possible for two men to have sex that way. So if being with Ted was exciting for me, it was also awkward and frustrating because I sensed it should have been much more than it ever was.

Once during spring break Ted was visiting me at home in Los Angeles. I was always very cautious around my family, but one night Ted and I came in very drunk, our arms around each other's shoulders, and fell into one of the twin beds in the back bedroom. The next morning my younger brother came in and looked at us in amazement, but nothing was ever said. If anybody had said anything we would have passed it off by saying we were drunk and didn't know or remember what we were doing. After all, that was how we explained, and justified, it to ourselves.

Thirteen

THE 1963 season was Kopay's best year at the University of Washington. The team went to the Rose Bowl at the end of that season. The school has not been represented in that game since then. The following summary of that year—Kopay's senior year—is taken wholly from the newspaper reports at the time.

Los Angeles Times—Sept. 16, 1963: Big Six football, team for team, is going to be vastly superior to that of 1962. As usual, Washington has the material for another fine football season. Senior Dave Kopay will attempt to fill the halfback void left by the graduation of Charlie Mitchell.

Denver Post—Sunday, Sept. 22: The gritty Air Force Academy Falcons ricocheted from repeated setbacks Saturday to upset the touted Huskies of Washington 10-7 before a screeching crowd of 23,542 at Falcon Stadium. Dave Kopay led the Washington ground attack with 37 yards on 10 carries.

Seattle Times—Sept. 26: John Stupey and Dave Kopay, senior lettermen, will be the University of Washington co-captains in Pittsburgh Saturday when the Huskies play the Panthers.

Seattle Post-Intelligencer—Sunday, Sept. 29: Junior quarterback Fred Mazurek scored one touchdown, passed for another and made two clutch defensive plays in the fourth period to lead unbeaten Pitt to a 13-6 victory Saturday over a stubborn Washington team. Mazurek's first game-saving effort came right after Washington scored its touchdown on Dave Kopay's 2-yard plunge.

Seattle Times—Sunday, Oct. 6 [by Georg N. Myers]:

Thunder, lightning, fumbles and fright struck the Huskies before a throng whose tears were as copious as the raindrops drumming its umbrellas. It was no fit day for football. But, 55,200 hardy, hopeful loyalists arrived swaddled for the monsoons, so the University of Washington and State University of Iowa fulfilled the commitment. The Big Ten chortled over a 17-7 triumph by the team appraised as the soft underbelly of the league. Dave Kopay, the senior halfback, sat on a bench after the game. He was partially dressed. The effort to continue seemed too much. "I don't think Iowa hit as hard as Air Force and Pitt. I don't know what happened."

Seattle Times—Sunday, Oct. 13: The University of Washington football team, after spluttering three weeks with a malfunctioning fuse, exploded yesterday 34-7 to blast Oregon State right out of Washington Stadium—and the undefeated ranks. It was the old Jim Owens on the sidelines. He leaped into the air, held his hands over his head and cheered, made a circle with thumb and forefinger to indicate "well done." Players tossed blankets into the air, and umbrellas sailed skyward in the student section. At game's end, the Husky band—with hats turned backward in victory symbol—went into the pavilion to serenade its team.

Seattle Post-Intelligencer—Oct. 14: The 439 yards gained against the Oregon State Beavers have catapulted Washington from fourth to first in Big Six total offense. Dave Kopay resides in ninth place (for individual rushing) with 124 yards at 3.6 yards a carry.

Seattle Times—Oct. 23 [by Bob Schwarzmann]: "Dave starts because he knows what we want to do," said Chesty Walker, the assistant coach who rides herd on Husky backs. "He plays sound, steady, dependable football. He has the best hands among the backs for receiving, and his speed is adequate. But to pinpoint it, the reason we have made some long runs is because of Kopay's blocking."

Kopay's face reflects his football career—rugged. The 6-foot-2-inch, 206-pounder was touted as, potentially, the best punter and place kicker in the school's history. He hasn't booted a ball since his sophomore season. The halfback's explanation was candid: "I lost my confidence after I had a punt blocked in the California game." Kopay earned a letter as a sophomore, but he was third string last year. "I wasn't fast enough." He didn't get a second monogram. "I like blocking—it's probably the best thing I can do. It feels good. I'm just one of 11 men working out there. We all know when we have played well. I'm wearing a purple shirt. That is what counts."

Seattle Post-Intelligencer—[Royal Brougham column]: Chitter Chatter . . . POME—Shake hands with a guy named Dave Kopay, he only knows one way to play; when the Husky halfback hits them right, they don't wake up till Monday night.

Seattle Times—Oct. 26:

TEAMMATES LAUD KOPAY

The Washington dressing room resembled Fourth and Pike on V-J Day. Rampant pandemonium. Mud-stained, the ecstatic Huskies thumped one another or just wandered with inane grins, trampling jerseys in the middle of the floor.

The chaotic uproar came to a focus at the end of the steamy, mucky room. There with a trickle of blood spotting his forehead, pale and tight-lipped stood Dave Kopay, almost unable to look up.

His running mate, Ron Medved, hoarsely whooped: "You just tell them. This guy played the greatest game I have ever seen anybody play. Kopay was great."

With emotion wrinkling his rough-hewn features, Kopay could only mumble. "I am sick of being pushed around by Oregon. We hadn't beaten them since I'd been at Washington."

Seattle Times—Nov. 3: The explosive University of Washington defense, keyed to a high-scoring line, yesterday thrust the Huskies into the center of the Rose Bowl scene by blasting Southern California's Trojans out of focus, 22-7. On the second play after the ensuing kickoff, Dave Kopay got his fingers on a Pete Beathard pass at the Trojan 32-yard line with only the horizon in his way. The ball slipped away. That moment of disappointment for Dave is mentionable, because it was the last detectable error by the craggy halfback acclaimed as the game's outstanding performer.

Los Angeles Herald-Examiner—Nov. 3: Southern Cal lost the game, but won a friend. Dave Kopay doesn't hate the Trojans anymore.

For one of Washington's biggest stars in the bone-crusher at Seattle yesterday, the 22-7 Husky victory wiped out the ill feeling the halfback from North Hollywood had for last year's national champs. In yesterday's *Herald-Examiner*, Kopay was quoted as saying: "I hate USC. I have ever since I was a kid. It's their attitude. Between the two schools down there, I was always a UCLA fan."

Apprised of the quote via the long distance wire, the Washington history major said in a sheepish tone: "Gee, I didn't think it would get in the papers at home. You can say I don't hate USC anymore. I respect them. The Trojans are the finest athletes I've ever played against. I really feel that way now that the frustration has been rubbed away."

The Washington co-captain was almost in tears as he appeared before the television cameras at the conclusion of the game with his coach, Jim Owens.

At the Kopay home in North Hollywood, Anton Kopay, father of the family hero, was joyous until the hamburgers began to burn. "I can hold my head up again," said the halfback's father. "I've been ribbed by so many people around here that SC is so great and that my boy's team didn't have a chance. I knew Dave would show them someday.

"The boys at Washington love the sweet smell of roses in their noses. So do I. Before the game, I went into the yard and plucked a Montezuma rose. I placed it on top of the television set, then watched the game. I've got to hang up now, the hamburgers are burning."

Valley Times—Nov. 4: Dave Kopay, who was too slow for Washington's 1962 backfield, was chosen AAWU back of the week today for his play in the Huskies' upset victory over USC Saturday. Kopay was a question mark as the Washington team was being made up this year. But he moved into the starting halfback spot on his slashing defensive play and spectacular blocking.

Kopay was honored for his sensational all-around play in which he scored one touchdown, set up the key block for another, carried the ball nine times for 25 yards and snagged two passes for 58 yards. Additionally, Dave intercepted a Trojan pass and made eight tackles.

Seattle Post-Intelligencer—Nov. 7: Never before have brotherly lectures created such devastating results. Periodically this spring, Tony Kopay, then a student-assistant coach at Washington, would dispassionately chide his younger brother Dave for inadequate performance.

"Tony got mad at me last year," Dave admitted with a half-smile. "But I had a lot of good boys ahead of me. I wasn't quite ready yet. Tony helped me a lot this spring. He never let me get down. I felt the guys ahead didn't belong there. Tony would say things to me. I'd get mad, but I knew what he was trying to do. He was trying to help."

UPI—Nov. 5: Jim Owens, who demands—and gets—physical conditioning from his players on a scale that probably would satisfy even President Kennedy, looked up and grinned sheepishly. "It is just a twinge in my back. Got it last Friday night." Owens admitted the twinge might have been aggravated when his happy warriors carried him off the field after they had upset the Trojans. And dunked him, suit and shoes, into the showers, "but it was worth it."

UPI—Berkeley, Calif. Nov. 9: The University of Washington Huskies, riding high on the road to the Rose Bowl, spotted California early leads twice Saturday, then came back to grind down the Golden Bears and win a wild 39-26 ball game. For 20 minutes after the victors stomped in, they listened with downcast eyes to a heart-to-heart lecture from their coach. "He told us he was happy we won but not happy with the way we won."

Los Angeles Times—Nov. 10:

WASHINGTON, 0 (NO FOOLIN')!! UCLA, 14;

UPSET SNARLS BOWL PICTURE

Mauled and pushed around most of the season, UCLA's Bruins rose to majestic heights at the Coliseum Saturday. Coach Bill Barnes' blue-shirted battlers shut out mighty Washington, 14 to 0 before 30,395 thrill-saturated spectators and thereby threw the Rose Bowl race in doubt.

Seattle Times—Nov. 24: A weekend free turned into a lost weekend for most of the University of Washington football team. "We're at loose ends," Chuck Bond, burly senior tackle from Puyallup, said yesterday. "We had one thing planned for today—and nothing else."

The one thing—the football game against the Washington State Cougars—was wiped out by postponement to next Saturday out of respect to the memory of President Kennedy. "The coach told us to forget about football," said Dave Kopay, senior halfback. "We can't forget football—just like that. But I'm sure we would have been in no mood to play football today."

Seattle Times—Dec. 1: A line is the shortest distance between two points—Seattle and Pasadena. The University of Washington frontmen proved that yesterday when they "defensed" the Huskies into the Rose Bowl with a 16-0 homecoming victory over Washington State before 56,000 fans in Washington Stadium.

Seattle Post-Intelligencer: The Huskies leave for their Rose Bowl engagement on Dec. 16. The team will work out twice a day at the facilities of Long Beach City College. Dave Kopay packed Bermuda shorts for his California "vacation."

Los Angeles Times—Dec. 17: It's no blind date the Washington Huskies are primping for with Illinois in the Rose Bowl. They've gone out together before. "I'm well acquainted with

Butkus, Sutton and the rest of their players," Coach Jim Owens said Monday after sending his Huskies through their first workout at Veterans Stadium in Long Beach.

Seattle Times—Dec. 16: Besides the training grind, the Huskies face an agenda of diversions, including an "all you can eat" dinner next Thursday, an excursion to Disneyland and the traditional Tournament of Roses Christmas party on Christmas Day. Nancy Kneeland, Tournament of Roses Queen, and her court of princesses from Pasadena Junior College, will be hostesses to the Christmas party.

Los Angeles Times photo caption: Rose Queen Nancy Kneeland is slightly aghast as she checks the king-sized portions of prime rib on the plates of Rick Redman and Dave Kopay of Washington.

AP Wirephoto caption: In Anaheim, Calif., yesterday, Washington's co-captains Dave Kopay and Mike Briggs were introduced to Mickey Mouse at Disneyland by Nancy Kneeland, Tournament of Roses Queen.

Los Angeles Times—Dec. 28: There's one on every team, and the "holler guy" on the Washington Huskies is an intense senior from North Hollywood—Dave (fastback) Kopay.

The 6-2, 205-lb. blond is always prodding his teammates, exhorting them to bear down, and he leads the cheers when they respond. When he says, "I used to think practice was work, but now I get a kick out of it," you know he means it. He likes to hit people, even his own.

AP Wirephoto caption: GAY BLADES/OLD TRADITION: Traditional University of Washington custom being observed in Rose Bowl as assistant coach Chesty Walker and starting backfield, Bill Douglas, Ron Medved, Dave Kopay and Charley Browning pick blades of grass from Rose Bowl end zone. They'll wear them in their belts today.

Seattle Times—Jan. 2, 1964: When Dwight D. Eisenhower and his wife, Mamie (radiant in a flaming red dress and hat) motored into the Rose Bowl in the grand marshal's limousine, they received a prolonged, standing ovation from the gallery.

Seattle Post-Intelligencer—Jan. 2:

HOORAY FOR KOPAY!

Dave Kopay, UW halfback, smashes between Illinois defenders to score a touchdown yesterday in Pasadena. All-American Dick Butkus of Illinois looks on from unaccustomed prone position. Siler pitched back to sweeping halfback Kopay. The pitch was high. Kopay grabbed it above his head, bent sharply and crashed the seven yards almost unhindered.

Los Angeles Times—Jan 2:

OWENS TOASTS "NEXT YEAR"

Jim Owens lost his first Rose Bowl game yesterday, but he did manage to set a new record yesterday afternoon. Owens kept the press cooling its heels for exactly 33 minutes after the final gun before appearing to post mortem the 17-7 loss to Pete Elliott and his Big Ten champion Illini.

Los Angeles Times—Jan. 2, 1964: Rose Queen Nancy Kneeland, 19, relaxed but "a little let down," was pulling petals from her bouquet of memories Thursday. There were a few thorns among her remembrances of the last month, too, but, best of all, one young fresh bud—the start of an apparent romance with Washington star halfback, Dave Kopay, 22, whom she dated Wednesday night.

Her blue-green eyes sparkled when she talked about her date. She and Dave attended University of Washington festivities at the Lafayette in Long Beach with his parents, Mr. and Mrs. Anton Kopay of North Hollywood.

While Nancy refused to call it a romance, her mother, Mrs. Erlene Kneeland of San Gabriel, winked. "I'm to meet the young man tonight," Mrs. Kneeland said.

UPI—San Francisco, Jan. 14, 1964: University of Washington halfback Dave Kopay signed up with the San Francisco 49ers of the National Football League, it was revealed yesterday. The Dallas Cowboys hit the scene about the same time that the San Francisco people did, but lost out as Dave figures he might have a better future with the California club. The Husky hero averaged 4.3 yards a carry this past fall and caught 12 passes good for 175 yards to lead his team in that department.

Seattle Post-Intelligencer—May, 1964 [Royal Brougham column]: ALUMNI GAME: Washington's gridders won a surprisingly hard-socking 10-0 victory over the Alumni in a game witnessed by 23,000. Dave Kopay, running like Northern Dancer, won this corner's vote for Player of the Day.

IV

Fourteen

IF the commissioner of the National Football League and the owners and coaches are overly sensitive about the public image of their players, it's surely because they're not about to take any risks with what has only recently become a major American profit-making enterprise. They may not know why after more than forty years of partially filled stadiums professional football is suddenly the most popular sport in America, but they can count.

College football was always popular in those same lean years. The big alumni "homecoming" weekends were never tied in with baseball or basketball, only football. Tom Dowling, in *Coach, A Season with Lombardi*, explains it this way: College football was where "young men were said to learn enduring lessons to prepare them for later life—sportsmanship, fair play, teamwork, second effort and so on. The college game was a sort of rite of passage, a young man's introduction to manhood in the panoply of a public spectacle. Moreover, the point of the college game was that it was played by young men who received no pay for their exertions and injuries. Money corrupted the moral content of the game, and it was this concept that blunted the success of the professional game for years. From the 1930s on, the pros were playing rougher, more exciting, and more adroit football than the colleges, but they were getting paid to play, and they were grown men, often in their thirties, who were acting out the transition to manhood years after the event was expected to have occurred."

David Kopay's decade with the National Football League coincided with the sport's "rise to dominance," as the NFL likes to call it. During Kopay's first year, 1964, the NFL signed the first of its big television contracts—with CBS for $14.1 million to broadcast two seasons. In 1976 NFL teams reportedly were paid in excess of $60 million for the telecasts of their games.

During the 1960s the confusion and upheaval in the rest of society only seemed to strengthen the authoritarian structure within the football world. David Kopay and his college team-mates heard the news of President Kennedy's assassination and went on in to watch the weekly game films as usual. The National Football League refused to postpone its games be-cause of Kennedy's death. In the face of several hundred thousand anti-war demonstrators during the 1969 morato-rium march on Washington, Vince Lombardi staged militaris-tic halftime shows at RFK Stadium in support of President Nixon and the war. One collaborator on this book was in a crowd singing, "Give peace a chance," outside the White House; the other was playing in the game the President was watching on television.

Dowling says in his book that the current appeal of football comes from the "nostalgia the game evoked, the suggestion of an orderly, disciplined past that was disappearing rapidly, the sense that only in sports were young people conducting them-selves in a truly American manner."

During the 1960's decade of social upheaval all of David Kopay's time and energy were spent staying in the game, and the passionate commitment he gave to the sport may help explain what so many Americans get out of it.

In *The Joy of Sports* (surely that is no innocent play on the title of the popular sex manual), Michael Novak talks of the feelings football arouses in him: "I find I cannot bear to have someone talk to me when I am concentrating on a game. At first I couldn't understand my own irritation; my nine-year-old would ask a question, a sensible question, and I'd hiss him into silence . . . During the game, my wife has noted, my palms sweat; impossible to gain my attention seriously. (I playact.) After the game, I am exhausted. Entertainment? It is more like an ordeal, an exercise, a struggle lived through. And not exactly vicariously."

Compared to the other sports, football is like real combat. The most dangerous activity ex-baseball pitcher Jim Bouton describes in *Ball Four* is shooting "beavers" from the top of the Shoreham Hotel in Washington. Kopay recalls his preparation for a game as a soldier would remember his careful, fearful attention to detail as he got his uniform and gear ready for battle.

"I always got to the stadium early to be sure I had plenty of time to get everything just right. I went to the same trainer, did everything just as I always did it before every game. Long after I had stopped believing in the church, I continued to go to the Catholic mass for the team because I didn't want to do anything different that might change my luck.

"I was never able to eat the heavy meal that was laid out for us. For some reason the coaches kept serving thick chunks of meat for us to eat the day of the game, even though they knew we couldn't possibly digest them before we started playing. I was sometimes queasy because of what I'd eaten—although I usually ate only scrambled eggs, toast and hot tea before a game—but others would be bent over the john heaving up all the heavy stuff they'd swallowed. When I was with the Forty-Niners, Matt Hazeltine told me he always ate Wheaties. Why? 'Because they go down easy and they come back up easy.'

"All of this had to do with fear—the fear of not doing your job right, of letting your teammates down, the real fear of getting hurt. The Washington Redskins and other teams I played for kept buckets of orange and lemon slices for the players to suck on. Our mouths were dry not from exercising because we hadn't done any. They were dry because of our fear. I guess this is much more complicated than just letting your team down or just being afraid of getting hurt. Unlike baseball, professional football has no minor leagues. If you don't go out and prove you can do it every game, you can easily be off the team by the next game.

"To this day my worst nightmares are about being late for practice or missing the bus for a game. In fact, I was never once late for a bus or for practice—in two years of high school, four years of college and ten years of professional football. But my anxiety over that still comes out in these dreams. In one dream, I arrive at a stadium and wander around lost, not able to find my teammates or the locker room where I'm supposed to get dressed. In another dream, I have overslept and I'm running to catch the bus just pulling out of sight."

Kopay was the "perpetual rookie" throughout his professional football career. Against all odds in a vicious elimination system, he made it to the pros and stayed there by sheer determination. "In pro football," as Thomas Tutko and William Bruns say in *Winning Is Everything and Other American Myths*, "even those who survive the rigorous weeding out process (one estimate is that pro football players are the best 1/10,000 of 1 per cent of those exposed to the game) can anticipate a career that averages only five years." Coming out on top of those odds was in itself a daily kind of reward. Just being there meant that Kopay was among the best in the world at his chosen sport.

There were twenty-four teams in the two leagues when Kopay signed on as a professional. Technically each of the teams had a full roster at the beginning of each summer's training camp. Forty veterans returned to fill forty positions. One NFL official estimates that the professional teams get scouting reports on as many as 1,700 college players each year. The hiring of players is controlled by a "draft" during which the teams take turns at the top college players up to twenty players per team. When the draft of college players was completed in December 1963, David Kopay's name was not among those who had been signed. However, he attracted enough attention later by scoring Washington's only touchdown in the Rose Bowl and playing a game praised by the sportswriters that the Dallas Cowboys and the San Francisco Forty-Niners offered him a chance to try out as a free agent.

Kopay decided on San Francisco because it was closer to his family and to his friends and fans in Seattle.

Coming on as a "free agent" is the most difficult route to a professional football contract. Usually there are less than twenty free agents signed by all the teams. At the beginning of summer training camp in those days there were nearly one hundred players trying out for the forty positions. That number had to be cut to sixty by August 1; to forty-nine three weeks before the season started and to forty-three two weeks before and down to forty by the start.

The Forty-Niners' training camp was at St. Mary's College about thirty miles from San Francisco. As in most camps, the rookies were housed on the third floor of the dormitory. They talked about the daily cuts as soldiers whisper of casualties. Kopay spoke of "the big cutlass." "Who died today?" others would ask. By the end of training camp, only seven rookies were left on the third floor. David Kopay was one of them.

Asked why he would submit to such a lifestyle—of curfews and bedchecks for men in their twenties and thirties and constant insecurity about the job itself—Kopay answers, "Why not? It was what I did best. For six months' work I couldn't possibly have earned a higher salary. Most important, though, it was what I enjoyed more than anything else in the world. And success really does have to have something to do with enjoying your work. Besides, in what other job do you have 60,000 people cheering you on?" . . .

As has been written of writers and artists it might also be that he was seeking from the world the love and recognition not available to him as a child.

Fifteen

As the feisty underdog, Kopay continued to be a favorite of the sportswriters during his professional career—witness these comments taken from the newspaper accounts at the time.

Seattle Times—Bob Schwarzmann column: The excitement bubbled through the telephone receiver: "I've made the team. There're only 40 on the team and I've made it. It's all a dream. It's one of the greatest things that ever happened to me."

Boiled down, Dave Kopay said he is a salary-drawing member of the San Francisco 49ers. Kopay played in every game last season at the University of Washington. He was named most valuable back in last spring's Varsity-Alumni game, as an alumnus. He played defense for the West last June in the All-America game in Buffalo, N.Y.

Dave reported to the 49er training camp this summer as a free agent. On the grounds at Moraga, Calif., were 43 veterans, 26 rookies. "I watched them lop off the draftees," Kopay said. "We called it The Big Cutlass. You never really knew if you were making the team—until the last cut. I don't think it has been so horribly difficult. I am faster and stronger than when I was in school."

If there is a question how the word "brashrookie" came to be, check Kopay's observation: "I think I could do better if I got the ball more."

Seattle Post-Intelligencer—Royal Brougham column: The free agent in pro football is the man nobody wants, a dark horse fighting for a chance, a grimly determined competitor who has to make it the hard, hard way.

Like Dave Kopay of the 49ers. Everybody passed him up in the draft but the popular Washington halfback had confidence in himself. He caught on with San Francisco on a make-good-or-else basis and hit the jackpot.

When injuries benched a couple of first-stringers, Kopay said, "Here I am coach, ready, willing and able."

Today he is the starting left halfback in the 49er lineup, an unsung rookie who is winning a home as a ball packer and pass receiver. No bonus baby, Kopay fast-talked his way into a uniform. Now he owns it and no man on the team wears it more proudly.

Kopay really won his spurs against Chicago recently. He practically stole the show—96 yards running, another 50 with five receptions. He has scored two touchdowns and reeled off one 18-yard gainer.

Here's how Dave looks at it: "It must be wonderful to be able to get a big bonus and fat salary when you sign a contract. I wasn't enough of a star at Washington to rate such treatment. But a fellow gets a lot of satisfaction out of starting without a rep and proving to himself and the coach that he is good enough to play on the team. I guess it just takes hard work and a little luck." Plus lots of determination and confidence.

Seattle Times—Georg N. Meyers column: The Wall Street bulletin that the New York Jets want to thrust $389,000 at Joe Namath, a nimble Alabamian, to play quarterback left David Marquette Kopay gasping for air.

"Three hundred what thousand!" Kopay exclaimed. "I guess I have to believe it, but it's unbelievable. I wish him luck." Kopay has just completed a rookie season as the leading ball-carrier for a professional football team which signed him, as a free agent, after the National and American leagues left him out in the cold in the draft.

Dave has a private suspicion that sneaking into the San Francisco 49ers' back door, almost unnoticed, was to his advantage. "I can say this," Kopay said. "If going to camp with a big price tag on your head creates animosity, I didn't have any enemies."

Friends and former teammates of Kopay at the University of Washington tactfully tried to express their doubts and advance condolences to Dave when he headed last July to the 49ers' proving ground at Moraga, Calif. "Everybody was very polite and thoughtful," Kopay said. "Everybody was worried I couldn't make it. From the first day of camp, I was confident I could."

Seattle Post-Intelligencer—Royal Brougham column: Final statistics from the 49ers show Dave Kopay not only led the team in rushing, but scored two touchdowns while catching 20 passes for 135 yards and ran back two kickoffs for 30.

Seattle Times—Bob Schwarzmann column: San Francisco, while getting ready for the present campaign, acquired John David Crow in a trade which sent Abe Woodson to St. Louis. The eight-year man moved into the starting backfield, ahead of Dave Kopay.

Dave finds little joy in being pushed down to the second string, but he did discover a silver lining. "I'm glad to see the 49ers didn't draft any backs. I guess it shows a little confidence in me."

Kopay, although he labels it a "disappointing year for me," has his moments. Against Minnesota last Sunday, Kopay had scored two touchdowns by the time San Francisco led in the second quarter, 21-3. The 49ers won, 42-24. Dave's first six points came when he recovered Ken Willard's fumble in the end zone. The ball got away from the 49er fullback on the line plunge. The other Kopay touchdown was on a 20-yard pass from John Brodie, quarterback.

John David Crow is Kopay's albatross. "The way John David is going, it's hard for me to get in," Dave said. "I carried as much in one game last year as I have all season this time. But it is great that the team is a winner."

Seattle Post-Intelligencer—Royal Brougham column: A Seattle visitor, Matt Hazeltine, the captain and slashing linebacker of the San Francisco 49ers, is the ultra modern businessman-football player, a far cry from the athletic bum of a couple decades ago. Hazeltine heaps praise on ex-Husky Dave Kopay. "He has more spirit than almost any man on our team and he's always in perfect physical condition. Our fellows love the guy."

San Francisco Examiner—by Bob Brachman, Oct. 20, 1966: It's rough being your club's leading rusher in your rookie season and then have to go into a kind of semi-retirement thereafter. But the San Francisco 49ers' Dave Kopay can "handle it" as long as the men keeping him on the bench are performers like John David Crow and Ken Willard. And also as long as he knows he's going to have some part in the action as Kopay undoubtedly will against the Detroit Lions at Kezar Stadium Sunday.

As one rival coach commented: "With those four mastodons, the 49ers are better equipped to put welts on welts than anybody in the league." Last week Atlanta defensive tackle Karl Rubke, a former 49er, pointed to various bruises on his body and identified each in turn as "Crow's" or "Willard's," "Kopay's" or [Gary] "Lewis'."

"You figure you can stay in there and slug it out with a couple of them," Rubke commented. "You figure you're getting wear and tear, but so are they. But when they have a couple guys like Dave and Gary coming at you fresh, you're in tough."

On the first play of the series that could prove the turning point of the 49ers' season and the first time he carried the ball against the Green Bay Packers, Kopay blasted through the middle for 25 yards. The game-deciding march carried 67 yards and Kopay, in four pops, picked up 42 of them.

It was the happiest moment blond Dave has enjoyed since 1964 when he took over as a starter after both J. D. Smith and Don Lisbon had been injured and became the first 49er free agent since Joe Perry in 1948 to win the S.F. rushing crown.

"Dave could be the best backup back in the league," says Coach Jack Christiansen. "It's darn reassuring to have him around. He could be a first stringer on a lot of clubs, either as a fullback or a halfback. He's a good pass blocker and receiver. He does the same things as Crow, except he doesn't have the experience."

Guard Howard Mudd, who shares an apartment with Kopay, says the word "dedication" fits Dave to a tee. "Lack of self assurance isn't one of his problems," adds Howie. "The guy is so intensely involved with what he's doing that his chances for success are pretty good. He doesn't avoid contact in any way."

Dave's intensity makes him a natural target for needling by other 49ers. But he can give as much as he takes.

Chico Enterprise-Record—March 29, 1967: It was an optimistic Dave Kopay who spoke to the Chico Rotary Club at the Elks Club yesterday. The former University of Washington star was signed four years ago as a free agent and stuck with the club. "All we have to do is get together and start winning," Kopay said. "For my money, we have the most balanced attack in professional football."

San Francisco Chronicle—by Darrell Wilson: Dave Kopay, the 49er halfback who suffered a torn cartilage in his right knee during Sunday's 13-10 win over the Raiders, was placed on injured waivers yesterday. Kopay, a four-year veteran who was the club's leading rusher in his rookie year of 1964, will be out for an indefinite time, perhaps for the season.

"We still have six running backs," said Coach Jack Christiansen.

At age six, dressed in white
for my first communion.

In the backyard of
our house in Chicago—
my brothers Gary, left,
and Tony, right,
with Thumper the rabbit.

My sister Marguerite,
dressed for her first communion,
and myself behind our house
in North Hollywood.

Marguerite outside her office
in Ketchum, Idaho, summer of 1976.

After confirmation, age 12.

Christmas time, seventh grade,
13 years old.

In Sunday suit
on the lawn in front of
the Claretian Junior Seminary.

The varsity basketball team
at the seminary.
I was a freshman—
second from the right, back row.

My freshman class at the seminary.

High school graduation, June, 1960.

Tony, Gary and myself
playing football in
our backyard when I was
a college freshman.

Myself and fraternity brothers,
including my friend
Ted Robinson,
in football jerseys
I "requisitioned" for them—
all trying to look tough.

Fraternity brothers
and dates.
My brother Tony,
extreme left,
is putting "horns"
on me, third from left.

My date and I
at the Theta Chi Formal
in January 1962
my sophomore year
at the University
of Washington

A cocktail waitress
I won a twisting contest
with in Los Angeles
my sophomore year
in college.

Before the Big W Club
initiation: fraternity brothers,
left to right,
Dave Kopay, Ray Mansfield,
Dave Phillips and Rick Redman.

Modeling wedding clothes
for the student newspaper,
the Washington *Daily*,
my senior year.

With Coach Jim Owens after we beat Southern Cal my senior year. I played 52 minutes, offense and defense, of the game that won the conference championship and sent us to the Rose Bowl.

December 31, 1963: the day before The Game in the Rose Bowl in Pasadena, California.

The University of Washington's starting team at the Rose Bowl, January 1, 1964. Left to right, front: Joe Mancuso, Mike Briggs, Gunnar Hagen, John Stupey, Rich Redman, Jake Kupp, Al Libke. Standing, left to right: Kopay, Bill Douglas, "Junior League" Coffey, Ron Medved.

The Rose Bowl Queen, Nancy Kneeland, and myself during the team's visit to Disneyland. (AP wirephoto)

Coach Lombardi and myself,
Number 40, during the
Washington Redskins game
with the New Orleans Saints
in New Orleans, 1969.
(Photo by Nate Fine)

Halftime at Kennedy Stadium
with Coach Lombardi
standing behind Kopay (seated)
in the locker room.
Other players, from left,
are Sonny Jurgensen, Frank Ryan,
Walter Roberts,
and Charlie Harraway.
(Photo by Nate Fine)

I had just arrived at
the Redskins training camp
and Coach Lombardi was
testing my leg strength
with an Exergenie. He knew
I had had an operation
on my knee, but I was careful
to put my good leg up first.
(Photo by Nate Fine)

Catching a swing pass from Sonny Jurgensen during the Washington Redskins game with the Dallas Cowboys in 1969. (Photo by Nate Fine)

From left, my aunt Sister Susan, my mother, and my Aunt Coletta after the Detroit Lions-Chicago Bears game at Wrigley Field, Chicago, 1968.

Getting dressed for practice in Husky Stadium the week before annual Varsity-Alumni Game at the University of Washington, May 1, 1976—my first appearance since publicly acknowledging my homosexuality.

Sixteen

WHEN John Brodie first started calling me "Psyche" it confused and angered me. Most nicknames in football are targeted at your weak points and at least start out as a way of embarrassing you. Coaches, for example, often use them to manipulate players into action by working on their insecurities.

Now here was Brodie getting on me for being so serious about the game, for getting so "psyched up" even at practice. But since I started out with less speed than the coaches thought a running back ought to have I figured I had to make up for it in spirit and aggressiveness, and actually I think the coaches—and even Brodie—liked my attitude. At least they seemed to accept me right away, which I figured meant I had a chance to make the team—they wouldn't have bothered getting to know anybody who wasn't going to last.

As things worked out I had Brodie to thank for a lot of help making the transition from college to professional football. And for helping me survive ten years in the pros I can thank the fact that I started out in San Francisco competing against and playing with some of the toughest people in the game—in particular David Wilcox and Matt Hazeltine.

Coach Jack Christiansen contributed his share too. A demanding coach, he wasn't a strict authoritarian like so many of the others, and I think he got at least as much out of his teams as some of those I played for later who seemed so unreasonably strict. Some teams called the Forty-Niners' training camp "the country club of the West," which was a laugh. It was just that we didn't have to go through so many of the silly routines that they did.

There is also a good deal of hypocrisy about what life in training camp is supposed to be as opposed to what it really is. They say there is no drinking, but players and coaches rush to the nearest bar as soon as practice is over. They say there are no women, but many players have regular girl friends they go back to every year in the towns near the training camps, and a lot of married players look forward to camp as a vacation from their wives.

On my third night in camp during my rookie year Brodie and Hazeltine and Charlie Kreuger invited me to go along with them to a bar in San Francisco. I was so excited that they had asked me to join them I doubt I would have refused even if I had been too sore to move, but I worried that we would never make it back by the midnight curfew. We did leave the bar in time to get back, but when Brodie decided to stop along the way for something to eat we were late getting in and I went to bed thinking that was the end of my pro career. I knew the least infraction was enough to send an untried rookie packing, but I also knew that stars like Brodie could usually get away with breaking all the rules in the book. I once saw Sonny Jurgensen—during a critical transition time for the Washington Redskins—so drunk at practice he couldn't pronounce the calls. The new coach, George Allen, just looked the other way.

When Christiansen mentioned our being late the next day he said there would be no fines but that if anybody else broke curfew again they'd do somersaults up and down the field until they wished they had never been born.

In San Francisco I poured all my energies into football and lived pretty much without any kind of social life. I did have sex a few times with a woman who was a regular sex partner of some of the other players. I got along all right with my room-mates. But these were not the kind of close friendships that last. I guess we were all just too preoccupied with the game itself to get into any kind of deeper relationships with each other.

116

For four years I lived within minutes of the great gay capital of San Francisco and never had a real homosexual experience. The only time I got even close was when I sent Ted Robinson the money to fly in for a weekend visit, paid for with my first paycheck, which I also used to buy my parents a color television set. Ted and I went out with some of my teammates—looking for women, we told ourselves. Of course, no women came between us and we went home, drunk, and fell into bed. It occurs to me now that of the countless times I went out with teammates looking for women, there were very few times when any of us took home what we were supposed to be looking for. But in those days I felt absolutely alone in my private sexual desires.

Just as in college Ted and I held and fondled each other but there was no real sex. When we woke up in each other's arms the next morning I wanted to go on with the foreplay from the night before. Ted was shocked: "What do you think you're doing?" And that was the end of it—until I saw him next in Seattle at a wedding reception for one of our fraternity brothers. We drank a lot of champagne and left the reception to go for a "nap" in our hotel room. Again, we were drunk and didn't talk about it afterward.

Ted was very patriotic, and after he had earned a master's degree in criminology he joined the Marines, competing in officers' candidate school the way he had with me on the basketball court. He told me that he loved the rugged training, and in a short while made captain. I often wondered if Ted's obsession with being a dominant figure in the military didn't at least partly have to do with his sexual repression. I know he wasn't making it with women. It could be that all that unused energy—I was pouring mine into sports—was coming out of Ted from his command position as a Marine officer.

It also seemed that the closer Ted and I got to any kind of real relationship, the further we drifted apart. When I had worked in Alaska and once when he had worked in Hawaii we exchanged letters every week. When he went to Vietnam—a move that even at the time made no sense to me—we didn't write each other at all. I did see him nearly every year when I would go back to Seattle—for two years as a student during the off-season and then for the week around the annual Alumni game in May. He would talk to me about Vietnam, but I still couldn't be convinced it was something to risk your life over. Incredibly to me at the time, though less so now, after one tour as a Marine officer Ted went back to the hell of Vietnam as a civilian engineer. We then didn't see each other for several years, by which time I was playing with the Redskins and Ted was working at the Pentagon.

One of the places I had sort of established as mine when I had come back to Seattle as a pro was a bar called Gabe's that I helped make a hangout for ballplayers and Theta Chi fraternity members. Whenever a friend was getting married or had a special date the owner would send over a bottle of champagne with a "this is on Dave Kopay."

A lot of the guys in Gabe's, in addition to figuring me for a bigshot, also decided I was a real lover because of my apparent conquest of a go-go dancer—they only knew the half of it. We were having a stag party at another restaurant where this lady was performing a sort of belly dance. Bright red hair done up high, big breasts halfway exposed, a tight slender body, she came down from her platform to sit at our table. When somebody told her I was a professional football player I got all of her attention even though I was mostly getting off on the good-natured ribbing from my friends. Having gotten in too deep to back off, I swaggered away with her to her hotel room, where she displayed all sorts of lubricants, with which she created all sorts of new and strange feelings, including those from a massage of my prostate with a special suppository-like lubricant. I liked the way it felt.

After that, whenever I would go back to Gabe's, my buddies would carry on about what I had pulled off with the sexy go-go lady. Not wanting to lose points with them—that was at least partly it—I took her to the team party after the 1966

Alumni game, and from there back to her hotel room. Again it was an exciting performance—her hands moving in and out and all over me—but there was something unreal about her with the thick make-up, the huge pile of teased hair. And this was the first time I had slept with anybody I didn't like or really know. By the next morning I just wanted to get out of that room fast as possible. She woke up, saw me pulling my pants up and said, "You're not going anywhere, buddy." She also said she had a pistol in her purse and she would damn well use it if I tried to make a run for it. I caught some skin in my fly as I jerked up the zipper and threw on my shirt. Somehow I made it to the hallway outside her door, terrified she would open the door and aim a pistol at me before the elevator came.

She didn't come after me and I never saw her again, but the call was close enough to make me think twice about going off with a sexy lady to impress my friends. Here I had almost gotten myself shot and I wasn't even having sex the way I really wanted to.

Although they had seen me with dates a few times my teammates knew I didn't have a regular girl friend. I suppose that was why, on a flight back from a game with the Green Bay Packers when John Brodie saw me reading a book, he said, "Hey, Dave, there's a really nice girl I want you to get to know." She turned out to be one of the stewardesses, very popular with all the players, very efficient in getting them beer and food on flights back from the games, always with a smile and a sweet innocent way about her no matter how demanding or obnoxious the players got. Her name was Mary Ann Riley [fictional name], a trim blonde with pretty, birdlike features and a fresh, rosy complexion. Mary Ann had graduated from a good women's college in the South—she had interviewed the poet-novelist James Dickey for a paper—and I enjoyed talking with her. By the time we landed we had made a date for that same night, and I waited at the airport—my teammates razzing me as they filed past—until

119

she had finished work. We went off to a nice restaurant north of San Francisco and proceeded to get high on wine and friendly talk.

I was very comfortable with Mary Ann from the first. Every time that I had been with a woman before there was always the fear that I wouldn't be able to live up to the image of the football stud in bed. Many of my heterosexual teammates have talked to me in recent years about the same problems. The fact that they were always going off with women didn't necessarily mean they were able to function in bed any better than I did. All of us had to live with the knowledge that in most ways we were no different from other men, but there was a publicized myth that we were able to perform better sexually because we were big tough football players.

Mary Ann talked about sex so that I had a feeling she wouldn't especially care if I got too drunk and so had an excuse not to make it once we got into bed. She made me feel at ease about it in advance. After dinner we went back to the apartment I shared with Dave Wilcox, an all-pro linebacker with the Forty-Niners. It was the first time I had ever brought a girl back to this apartment, and I made certain to leave the lights on and the door open so that the event wouldn't go unnoticed. When Wilcox came in later that night he stopped, looked in and did a double take. A week later my teammates would still be razzing me about the "stew" I had made it with. And I would enjoy it, I would be one of the guys in every way—or so it would seem.

I had thought Mary Ann was innocent, but when we got ready for bed that first night she produced a kind of lubricant that turned into foam. She had no inhibitions about oral sex. The first night I was aroused enough by her to have an orgasm through intercourse. The next morning, though, I wasn't aroused by her at all—and yet I felt an obligation to have intercourse with her because, regardless of her seemingly relaxed attitude, I thought that was what she expected from a macho football player. I felt inadequate and frustrated that I

120

wasn't naturally aroused by her. I made several attempts but the feeling just wasn't there. The only way I could keep an erection was by masturbating, which I had never imagined doing with a woman. Surprisingly this didn't bother her at all—in fact she encouraged it, and later in our relationship it became pretty much the sum of our sexual relationship. She did seem to enjoy it, but I could never shake loose from the feeling that I should have been doing much more to satisfy her needs.

Through all of this I think I knew I would have been more aroused by another man, but the fact was I still didn't consciously know how to go about it. And certainly at the time I didn't think of myself as a homosexual any more than Ted did. Homosexuals were the effeminate "fags" or "fairies" of my teammates' curses. I had a long way to go before I learned the stereotypes weren't always true, that I was in truth a homosexual, and that I wasn't the only athlete who was. I had successfully blocked out so much of the sexual content of my relationship with Ted that I had never really thought in practical terms of how it could be more fulfilling. And not being able to fulfill my sexual relationship with him had, I believe, much to do with the anxiety I felt with Mary Ann. I would have been more relaxed with her if I had first been able to relate honestly with Ted.

After our first date Mary Ann wrote me a note saying she had enjoyed our night together and hoped we could do it again. I may have called her once or twice, but I didn't see her again until I was playing for the Detroit Lions.

It was my fourth year with the Forty-Niners. My parents were up for the game, which we had won. Afterward, I collapsed in the locker room and grabbed at my leg, yelling to John David Crow that my knee was locked. A doctor examined it and said I had torn the cartilage. I went into the hospital that night and was operated on the next day.

Only one of my teammates—and none of the coaches—

visited me in the hospital. The one who did come stayed only long enough to drop off a hooker he had met in a go-go place. She came back several times, usually bringing a bottle of wine, and was pleasant company, but we never went beyond conversation.

There was a tradition behind the failure of my teammates and coaches to come calling. An injured player is worse than a wounded soldier in combat. The player—unless a shot of novocaine can get him back in play—might as well be dead. Even in college we were taught not to look back if one of our teammates went down. The line of scrimmage was shifted and the injured player was left where he fell, to be taken care of by trainers and doctors. To be knocked out of play, of course, is death to a football player because you are only alive—as far as the game is concerned—when you're out there doing it. Otherwise coaches and teammates can't be interested in you. In fact, they have a real superstition about getting near someone who is out of play, as if the torn cartilages and broken bones were contagious.

At the time I was injured I was still negotiating my new contract with the Forty-Niners. They had made me a verbal promise of a specific raise, but once I was operated on they changed it to a figure $8,000 less than promised. I had a talk with John Brodie, who had just won a breach of contract suit with the league and signed a million dollar contract with the team, and his lawyers helped me get the contract settled in my favor. After five weeks' recuperation I made it back and finished out the season with the Forty-Niners. I was traded to the Detroit Lions for a third and fourth round draft choice, which did mean a step up in salary as well as status—after all, they considered me a better bet than two of the top incoming college players.

Lions Fanfare—spring edition, 1968: LIONS ADD VETERAN KOPAY. A swift- and hard-running halfback has been added to the Lions' roster for 1968. Injured last year, David Kopay saw limited action but carries a 3.7-yard rushing average. "I'm happy to have him," says Coach Joe Schmidt. "Kopay always has played well against us. He weighs 220, is a fine blocker and is one of those guys who gives 100 per cent all the time."

The Detroit News—August 27, 1968: Now, Kopay is the Lions' starting halfback in tandem with Mel Farr. "I thought I would be traded by San Francisco when I didn't play after being around three years," he says. "I was very happy to leave. Here, I'm playing. I'm starting."

Kopay has been well worth the price of the trade with 86 yards rushing and a touchdown in two games.

70th Division News—Fort Leonard Wood: "More P.T., sergeant!" is a familiar and factious request of Army trainees to their drill instructors during exercises. Among the ranks of the 70th Division (Training), now at Fort Leonard Wood for their annual two weeks of summer training, there is one soldier that means it when he asks for more "physical training."

He is Private First Class David M. Kopay, currently a member of the Detroit Lions team. He will be starting his fifth season as a professional player. "I don't keep in shape just for football or the Army. I do it because you feel much better," Kopay added. "You can cope with whatever you have to do each day when you're in top shape physically and mentally."

Detroit Free Press—The Inside of Sports by Joe Falls, sports editor, July 13, 1969: It was very still and quiet at Cranbrook School. Two men were alone out on the practice field. "What'll it be?" said Bill Munson.

Dave Kopay, still huffing and puffing from the last pass pattern, looked down at the ground with his hands on his knees, trying to catch his breath. "Flare left," he said.

Munson walked up to the imaginary center and started calling off his signals: "Thirty-two . . . twenty-nine . . . hut-hut!"

He took the imaginary snap and started backtracking as if the pressure was on. Kopay ran down about 20 yards, cut to his left and Munson fired a bullet into his arms, and Kopay took off for another touchdown.

Our boys return this week with the rookies and some of the veterans reporting to Coach Joe Schmidt for dinner Tuesday night. Munson and Kopay couldn't wait. They were holding their own camp and it was like all football camps in the summertime. It was damn hard work.

The perspiration flowed freely from both men, saturating their faces and discoloring their sweatshirts. For Kopay, this is a very important season. He is hoping to make it back from a knee operation and two foot operations, and he was running his patterns as if indeed he was trying to beat Rick Volk of the Colts.

Seventeen

ALEX KARRAS of the Lions was a
legendary figure to me long before I got to Detroit. One of my
roommates and best friends in San Francisco, all-pro offensive guard Howard Mudd, had talked about Karras as one of
his lifelong heroes.

So when I was first introduced to Karras it was like meeting
the embodiment of some mythical character. He and I and
quarterback Bill Munson became instant friends. One reason
had to be that the Lions had traded for Bill and myself to
strengthen their offense. Alex himself had always been a star,
but Detroit's weak offense had left him as an outstanding
player on a losing team. He saw in Munson and me some new
hope for a winning season. Coach Schmidt sometimes called
us "The Three Musketeers." It was probably the first time
Alex had been friends with the quarterback, and it seemed
that he was making a genuine effort to put the team effort
ahead of his own stardom.

Alex never seriously kidded me about the lack of women in
my life and didn't really seem to care one way or the other,
but sometimes he would say, "I don't believe you, you should
have all the ladies you want." At other times he would laugh
and say, "Maybe I'm not the only Greek around here." Which
was when I would panic, hoping he wouldn't carry the joke
any further.

He called me "Stash" because, he said, I dressed like an
immigrant. Actually his wardrobe was about as lean as mine,
and he would joke that he was "just a beer-drinking steel-
worker from Gary, Indiana." He was a damn sight more interesting, more complicated than that. He stood six feet one

125

and weighed more than 255 pounds. Without lifting weights, he was one of the strongest men I ever knew in professional football.

My friendship with Alex was all that kept that season from being a painful, completely frustrating one for me. I had injured my knee again, the same knee but another torn cartilage. For the whole year I would need to have the knee drained on Fridays before the games and again on Mondays afterward.

Alex, Bill Munson and I hung out at a place called Larko's. Pete Larko, the owner, was a special friend of Alex's and never let us look at the menu or pay a cent. The Larkos would just bring out heaping bowls of food until we were stuffed. Alex could eat an incredible mound of spaghetti, enough for a whole family. We spent a lot of time with Pete and his older brother Nick Larko, talking and playing gin for hours, and if anybody began giving me a hard time about not having a girl friend Nick was quick to tell them to "leave him alone."

Two of Larko's waiters were openly gay—I had never been in a situation where as football players we were in contact with gay people—and Pete Larko would laugh with them and sometimes kid them about being gay but it was always in good humor. I was sure he would never demean or ridicule them behind their backs. This meant a lot to me.

Three or four times Alex asked me to go along when he and a friend had "a scene going" with prostitutes in a motel room. From his description of the women I wasn't interested in them, and although I liked Alex as a friend I wasn't sexually attracted to him. I always passed on these scenes. Similar ones I've been in seemed to me examples of men relating to one another and using the woman as an excuse.

They called me "Junior" in Detroit, meaning Alex, Jr., and while I at first resented it, after a while I decided I liked being associated with Karras. My association with him, though, made me all the more fearful about my homosexuality—I figured that if anybody found out it would also reflect on him.

Two linebackers, Wayne Walker and Mike Lucci, were especially rough on me, and I didn't think they were kidding. They were the ultimate in macho football players and they really gave me a rough time—or at least I thought they did at the time. It could be that I was over-sensitive then, plain terrified they would find out about my suppressed homosexual feelings. I'm not sure either of them ever used the word "fag," but I was sure that was what they meant each time they needled me about not having a date, and then when they saw I was upset stepped up the cracks and insinuations.

Anxious as I was about being secretly homosexual, I wondered about the hypocrisy of some heterosexual players who on the one hand claimed to have ideal happy marriages and on the other were competing as fancy dressers and carrying on about their extra-marital conquests. It wasn't much comfort, but at least, I figured, if all wasn't right in my private world, it wasn't exactly perfect in theirs either.

Things really evened up between "them" and me at practice—my most acceptable opportunity to strike back at these guys—and, believe me, I loved it. They knocked me around plenty too, but it was a great feeling to know I could stand up to the toughest of the tough. Make all the cracks you want in the bars, I thought, but you're going to respect me on the field. I think they did.

As a matter of fact I respected Walker and Lucci as players. There was a particular pass-blocking drill where I faced these two direct and head-on that helped build this mutual respect. My pass blocking was the main reason the Forty-Niners had kept me for four years, and I was very aggressive at it. Lucci weighed about 235, Walker about 225. I wasn't exactly pint-sized at 220. This drill usually attracted most attention during practice because it was such a clear test of a player's courage and experience. We were taught to block with our heads, which meant you'd better develop a strong neck or you'd get it broken.

To carry out a blitz on the quarterback—the purpose of the

drill—the linebackers had to get through a three-yard-wide lane. On the count of hut two or hut three the backs would move into a more protective position. Bags were set up to represent offensive guards, tackles, center and ends. The linebackers had to run through the narrow lanes between them.

My job was to protect the quarterback. If I hesitated or drifted backward, the linebackers could easily run over me. But if I charged ahead—knowing when the ball would be snapped—I could build a momentum of my own and stop them in their tracks. I got a special pleasure out of smashing into Walker and Lucci when they would come at me, the memory of their cracks providing extra fuel for my counter-charge. There were no comments about my sex life when they were picking themselves up off the ground.

Some of the Lions stayed at the Leland Hotel in downtown Detroit, and its Hideaway Bar was a hangout not only for the women and businessmen who never seemed to get enough of hanging out with football players, but also for a number of gay men.

Maxine Werby, whose husband was one of the hotel's owners, was a large, friendly lady who loved to sit and drink with the ballplayers. She also had friends among the gay people who visited her in the bar. She told me about taking a group of football players to see a female impersonator and that I really should have been with them. I quickly said I didn't want to see anything like that, and she just as quickly said, "Oh, yes you do."

I eventually did go with Maxine, three other ballplayers and a gay musician, expecting a performance like the ones my buddies had talked about at Finnochio's in San Francisco, where, they said, the impersonators were so glamorous they would have gone for them never mind what they were. But this night in Detroit we went to a grundgy little bar where a fat old guy in a dress was the "entertainment." We stayed through his routine, went back to the hotel and the other players took off, leaving Maxine, her friend and me sitting together in the bar.

"We've got another place we want to show you," Maxine said, and her friend added, "Come on, it'll open your eyes to a lot of things."

I agreed, figuring I was ready for anything after the last place. We went over toward the river to an area that had been leveled for new high-rise buildings, leaving only one old building sitting there as if it had survived a bombing raid. I still had no idea where they were taking me, but at least the guys in front of the old building didn't seem different from those I had seen at the hotel bar.

When we pushed on into the bar, I was stunned. There was a huge dance floor, jammed with people—all of them men. I turned and glared at Maxine and her friend. "How the hell do you have the nerve to bring me to a place like this? If you don't take me back, I'm walking back." They never asked me to go to their bars again.

I realized that Maxine could see that I was hiding my homosexuality, and I suppose that's why I panicked in that bar. I knew I looked like the other football players and there was nothing wrong with my performance on the field, but there was still something about me that had told her I was secretly homosexual. And if she could detect this, was it possible other people could too? I could see myself ruined as a professional football player. I could see this as the end of my friendship with Alex Karras.

It was not an unfounded fear. A year or so later when Alex knew for certain that I was homosexual, he eased away from me and has never been more than polite since. True, he never made any cracks to me, but sometimes he does now on television when he talks about the Greek Cypriot looking at him in the shower, when he jokes that what he misses most about football is showering with the guys, laughing about one player's earring and another's hairdo.

In Detroit I had finally been put in contact with other gay people—although none that I knew were athletes—and in the process was getting closer and closer to recognizing my true sexual identity.

After that season in Detroit I had to have another operation on my knee, and when this time I didn't heal so quickly I went home to Los Angeles to recuperate. Back in Detroit for training camp at Cranbrook School the next summer, I thought I had made the team, but two weeks before the season started I was traded to the Washington Redskins, who had just finished their first training camp under Coach Vince Lombardi.

I was very excited about playing under Lombardi. I had heard how tough he was, but I had also heard that he treated his players fairly. For a running back my speed was anything but spectacular (4.9 seconds in the 40), but I knew Lombardi had played many backs who weren't much faster. For once I thought I would be playing for a coach who looked at my performance and not at his stopwatch, and I figured the fact that his training was so rough had to be to my advantage—I could show him what I could do if given a chance.

I also felt I would get a chance to play regularly in Washington because the team just didn't have any veteran backs on my level. In San Francisco I was always behind John David Crow and Ken Willard; in Detroit I was behind Mel Farr and Altie Taylor. I didn't know it, of course, but coming along were two great young players named Larry Brown and Charlie Harraway. And when I was aware of them I still felt that my ability to play halfback and fullback and my experience on all the special teams would keep me in action under Lombardi.

Washington offered me another chance to start over, a chance to prove myself once again as a football player. It was also the place where I would finally have to deal with my identity not just on the field but off as well.

Eighteen

To those tourists who see only the sterile government buildings and the bureaucracies they hold, Washington, D.C., might seem an unlikely setting for a professional football player's advance to sexual liberation.

The truth is Washington in the last decade has become one of the most pleasant places to live in America. There are colorful beds of flowers and green spaces in almost any direction you look. There are no tall buildings towering over you. There is a sense of space, a nice feeling that there is room to move around in, a place where you can be yourself without harassment from others who might disagree with you or your lifestyle. It is the only American city designed with beauty as the prime consideration, instead of commerce and industry. There are bike trails in a dozen directions—along Rock Creek, on both sides of the Potomac and along the towpath beside the old C & O Canal. Coming back down the towpath there is a point where the spires of Georgetown come into view, highlighting a mellow scene as picturesque as anything to be seen in the villages of old Europe.

And while people may still argue about how it looks, they cannot argue with the success of the Kennedy Center of the Performing Arts, the hub of a busy cultural scene that made Washington—almost overnight—second only to New York as a center of cultural diversity. In fact Martin Duberman's play about male hustlers, *Payments*, couldn't find a stage in New York but opened at an experimental theater in Washington. It wasn't an unusual night when Nureyev and Tennessee Williams were seen dancing at a gay discotheque in Georgetown, and the gossip columnists were moved to only passing mention when rock singer Elton John toured the bars and discotheques another night. An evening in Georgetown might include drinks with, say, opera singer Beverly Sills, dinner with such writers as William Burroughs, Allen Ginsberg and Larry McMurtry, the novelist, who owns a rare book shop in Washington. And the emergence of *The Washington Star* as a lively, literate afternoon counterpart to the morning *Post* has given the city the highest level of competitive journalism of any city in America.

For a variety of reasons, Washington is about as congenial to the gay people who live there as any other city in America. Perhaps this is related to the coincident rise of interest in music and theater in the city; or to the heavy concentration of highly educated people who work there; or to the fact that a majority of the population and almost the entire city government is composed of black people, who generally tend to look on another minority with compassion because of their own history of being oppressed. Whatever, the general feeling seems to be that in Washington—where the government, the public, is the chief employer—a person's private life should be just that. This isn't to say that the gay community in Washington lives completely without harassment, but that more progress has been made than in most cities of comparable size toward a situation in which people are not discriminated against because of their sexual preference.

When Henry Kissinger bought a townhouse in Georgetown he was reputed to have objected to the gay men walking by outside it—he had located himself, his wife, dog and attendant Secret Service men square in the middle of what has been the gay-cruise block in Washington since 1945. Mrs. Huntington Block—whose back garden is adjacent to the Kissinger property—feels differently, as she told *The*

Georgetowner: "I love them dearly. I feel safe. My children love them. They saw some burglars wheeling some of our plants out of our house this summer while we were away and called the police, who caught them. I like having people there, whatever kind of people they are. It's comfortable."

Georgetown, a river port long before the federal district was laid out over and around it, is a lovely old residential section of narrow, tree-lined streets with mossy brick sidewalks and ivy-covered townhouses, each with a small garden in back. It was here, in September 1969, that the new Redskin running back David Kopay decided he would live, and moved into a townhouse in the heart of Georgetown with his new teammate, Bob Long.

After a few nights in and around Washington, Bob Long and I both decided on Georgetown as the place where we wanted to live. During my entire four years with the Forty-Niners I had lived in Redwood City twenty-five miles from San Francisco and had never gotten to be any part of the life there. The residential part of Georgetown reminded me of the older parts of San Francisco, with a lively nightlife centered on the singles bars along M Street that Bob and I both enjoyed. And, from the first, I could see that a number of gay people were also accepted as part of that scene.

It must seem ironic to some of my ex-teammates now that at the time they thought I was making a mistake sharing a house with Bob Long. They thought he was effeminate in his gestures and the way he ran, and in camp fashion would tease him with an "Oh, you big *bruiser* . . ." Long, secure in his private life as a ladies' man, would shrug off the remarks and say, "That's just the way I run." He had the last laugh when after he retired he opened a chain of bars and restaurants and called them "Bruiser's."

Long had started his career playing for Green Bay in 1964,

then in 1968 was traded to the Atlanta Falcons. He was leading in pass receptions there until an oncoming car crossed
over the median on an interstate highway and crashed into his
car, breaking his right foot, knee cap, hip, three vertebrae
and right elbow. Coach Lombardi, unimpressed with these
injuries, called up Long when he took over the Redskins and
managed to convince him he could play again. Lombardi,
after all, had once told a player he could play on a broken leg
because the bone involved was not a "weight-bearing bone."
Amazingly, during that season with the Redskins Long ranked
fourth in the NFL in pass receptions.

I didn't know it at the time but before I was signed the
Redskins had fired a player thought to be homosexual. Hiring and firing players in the NFL is such a subjective process—coaches and owners are pretty much unaccountable
for their decisions—it's difficult to say even now with cer-
tainty that homosexuality was the reason this player was cut
from the team. He had, though, been an all-American in college and a top Redskins draft choice that year. The Redskins
had also investigated rumors of his homosexuality before
they signed him on and apparently had satisfied themselves
there was nothing to them. "I will not let these unfounded
rumors keep such a talented player from playing," the team's
owner, Edward Bennett Williams, told a colleague.

That same year one of the Redskins major stars was stopped
by police for driving drunk the wrong way down a one-way
street, and another time was caught having sex with a woman
in a car parked beside Anthony House, a hotel just a few
blocks from the park where the other incident took place.
None of these incidents was officially reported by the police,
nor were they ever reported in the newspapers. The heterosexual incident was joked about and forgotten.

Ray Schoenke, now a successful insurance man in
Washington, was playing swing man on the Redskins line that

year and knew this player, and while some people told me the player was "outrageous" in flaunting his homosexuality, Ray and several other Redskins said he was no different in his behavior from the others on the team. Ray also told me that Sonny Jurgensen was "brutal" about this player's homosexuality, calling him a "goddamned fag" or a "cocksucker" every time he made any kind of mistake.

I had heard these stories about Jurgensen from other players, and later wondered why he would taunt this particular man when he never did it to me or to another homosexual player who had been on the team some years before I arrived. Maybe it was because this player was also black—"fag" was acceptable, "nigger" was not. More likely—though I'm still guessing—Jurgensen got on the guy because he wasn't a super performer. As the first black players soon learned, race was overlooked as long as they contributed more to the team than the average white player. It is interesting that the other homosexual Redskin—never openly taunted by his teammates—was both white and one of the best players at his position in the NFL.

Tom Dowling in *Coach, A Season with Lombardi,* describes the homosexual player who was cut and Coach Lombardi's reaction to him:

"Professional football is not a world like the theater or the ballet, where sexual deviations are shrugged off. Love beads and long hair are considered depraved by the average football coach and homosexuality a crime of almost unspeakable dimensions. There was a player on the Redskin roster who was widely reputed to be a homosexual. I could not envy the man the physical skill that had led him into professional sports as a livelihood. His life would be one of ill-concealed smirks when he entered the shower room and of occasional challenges to fight like a 'man.'

"I was authoritatively told that the player's 'problem' had

come up at a coach's meeting in a less than charitable fashion. Lombardi was reported to have winced and said that he had never felt so strongly about a player making the club. He had said that he hoped he could help in some way by showing that he, at least, was in the player's corner. One of the assistant coaches had said that he thought placekicker Charlie Gogolak, a Princeton man, was probably treated worse by the team because of his Ivy League background. No, said Lombardi, Gogolak was a lawyer, a smart kid with everything going for him. The other kid had nothing going for him, and he worried what the player could do to make a living if he couldn't make it in professional football.

"Football is a 'man's' game, and as such its borders were sketched in boyhood with its herd mentality. There were not many men in professional sports who had spent a lifetime in that atmosphere and had risen above it. In many areas, Lombardi had."

Dowling now says that this was no isolated incident. He says there is no question that Lombardi, the owners and the other Redskin coaches knew about this player's homosexuality. What turned Lombardi against the player, Dowling believes, was his inability to become the player Lombardi wanted him to be. "Had he been a great player, he would have played regardless," says Dowling. "Few coaches are going to dump a class ballplayer just because he is discreetly homosexual. I'm sure you know as well as I that there are numerous homosexual players in the NFL. Their coaches know it as well and these men are still playing. They know exactly who gave those anonymous interviews to the *Star*."

According to Dowling, a player's behavior would only be an issue if it became a public scandal. The Dallas Cowboys, he says, were aware that Lance Rentzel had been caught exposing himself to a young girl before they hired him. The owners and coaches apparently only got upset when another incident was reported in the newspapers.

136

Ed Garvey, executive director of the NFL Players Association, says the association would defend a player dismissed because of his homosexuality. Although there has never been such a case, he says this would be consistent with the association's position that the league and the franchise owners have no right to interfere in a player's private life. He points out that the association did defend Rentzel "and that's about as extreme a situation—in the public's mind—as you can get regarding sex."

There are others besides Dowling who feel that the homosexuality of the player cut by Lombardi—apparently he didn't seek any legal recourse—didn't figure in his dismissal. Somebody close to Lombardi at the time says the homosexual player was actually the coach's favorite at the beginning of training camp, but could never manage to run the way Lombardi wanted. Instead he insisted—as if stubbornly trying to prove his courage with every play—on running straight up, and so exposing his upper body to injury. Lombardi could never get him to bend over so that his helmet and shoulder pads could protect him the way they were supposed to. The player also came up with an injury in his Achilles tendon that was slow to heal. As a marginal player with the Redskins his homosexuality might finally have had some influence on Lombardi's decision to drop him—if for no other reason than the friction it caused between him and the star quarterback Sonny Jurgensen.

As authors of this book, Perry Young and I wrote to Edward Bennett Williams, still the chief owner of the Redskins, asking for an interview to discuss generally the question of rights of homosexual players in the National Football League and the specific circumstances involving this player's being cut in 1969. Williams, also lawyer for *The Washington Post* and treasurer of the national Democratic party, gave us this one-sentence answer: "I have neither interest in, information about nor time to discuss your client's homosexuality."

Williams once spoke with pride about how he refused to buy into the then all-white Redskins in the early 1960s because "I just can't be part of an organization that's the last bastion of discrimination." It would seem that he doesn't recognize the similarity between discrimination against a person because of race and discrimination because of sexual preference.

We also tried for several months to locate the player himself. None of his former teammates and nobody at the NFL Players Association offices in Washington had any idea what had happened to him. The lawyer in Seattle who helped negotiate his $70,000 three-year no-cut contract hadn't heard from him in years, and neither had his best friend in college, although he did say he had heard something about him from a mutual friend during a visit to the town where they had both gone to college. The other friend, a postman, and his wife had given parties for the football players in those days and had tried to keep in touch after the players left school. He said that this particular player was now working as a school monitor in a southwestern town. The school was called. Yes, there was a man who fitted the player's description, but he had a different name. Nobody with that name had ever worked at the school. The man's friends said that they would not be surprised to hear that he had changed his name. "Of course," one of them added, "we didn't care that he was homosexual, but I guess he never knew that." He couldn't have known that because none of them ever told him.

"Homosexual" was hardly a foreign word in the Washington football environment I moved into early in September 1969. I had heard rumors not just about the homosexuality of the player who had been dropped but about other players too, including an all-pro who as of 1976 was still a player.

It would be in Washington that I would finally confront all of the sexual anxiety and confusion of my past. My stewardess friend, Mary Ann Riley, was living in Washington. And so was my college friend, Ted Robinson. Just as important, there was the city itself, where I was free to roam around, in search of myself, away from my teammates and the myths they—and I—had lived by.

Nineteen

EXCITED as I was at the prospect of playing for Lombardi, being sent to the Redskins after I thought I had made the team in Detroit was, at first, hard to take. I wasn't surprised, though, that Lombardi had picked me up—I had always played well against his teams, especially when the Forty-Niners tied Green Bay in the last quarter and forced them into a playoff with Baltimore, and an all-around good game with the Lions against Green Bay.

I had already been briefed by a friend, Walter Rock, a teammate at San Francisco before he went to the Redskins, about how especially rough training camp had been that year, but I didn't worry about it. And besides I knew, with the season just about to begin, practice couldn't be all that rough, at least not for the next few days. As it turned out my timing, and my logic, were badly off.

I got to Washington on a Friday night and the next day the Redskins were beaten in an exhibition game. Lombardi was outraged. He ordered two practices a day when normally by then they would have been down to one. Coming as I did from the cooler climate of Michigan, the hot, humid weather of Washington was something else. That first morning's practice under Lombardi was the roughest thing I had ever known in football—and I hadn't even helped lose the exhibition game. He put us through non-stop, twenty minutes to a half-hour running exercises. We did endless "upsy-downsies," agility moves, turning, stopping, turning and jumping. After we finished our regular practice schedule he lined us up and drilled us in plays the length of the field until we got them down letter-perfect. The offensive teams ran the plays, and the defensive teams ran straight ahead. Lombardi put us out 20, then 30, then 50, then 100 yards, and we had to keep running those plays to the goal.

My guts were aching, my legs were so wobbly I was afraid I would fall. I was dizzy and worried that my knee was going to give out. I kept going, though, because I knew the only kind of player Lombardi liked was one who would "play hurt," even with broken bones if he had to. Nobody would have been caught dead in the training room under Lombardi. Your injury was either so bad you had to be carried off in an ambulance—or you played.

I had a good week of practice, and I made the team.

Even when I believed in Lombardi and would have done anything to please him I think I also realized that there was something cruel about the way he manipulated his players. I was "Attaboy, Dave" as long as I was doing well—or rather as long as he thought I was doing well—but then about midseason I dropped a pass and he never had a good word for me after that.

When I arrived in Washington, though, I had the gung-ho aggressive spirit of a young rookie. That year Lombardi was also out to prove himself again. Two years before he had announced his retirement in Green Bay. Now he had come to Washington to take a losing team and make it into a champion the way he had done in Green Bay. He started things off at an introductory banquet for the team at the Shoreham Hotel with a really powerful speech. The fans and my teammates seemed to share a genuine enthusiasm I had never felt before with a professional football team. It was great being identified as one of Lombardi's men—there was a new spirit about the Redskins in Washington that year, and it all had to do with Lombardi's arrival as coach.

The Evening Star—Morris Siegel column: Unless he has sprouted two or three inches since the official NFL tape measure was used on him, Dave Kopay, latest Redskin hopeful,

141

doesn't quite measure up to Vince Lombardi's specifications. Lombardi says the ideal foot soldier should be about 6 feet 2 or 6 feet 3. However, Kopay is close enough to merit critical observation, considering the qualitative scarcity of running backs at Fort Lombardi.

Kopay becomes the 13th or 14th ball carrier for the Redskin screening committee to pass judgment on. Although he was unwanted by the Detroit Lions, he could become the cream of the Redskin crop. Kopay, as suggested, fails Lombardi's altitude standard by two inches but goes about 10 pounds more than his displacement requirement. Now let's go all the way with Dave Kopay.

Washington Daily News—Nov. 26, 1969: "Our specialty teams are killing us," Vince Lombardi moaned after Washington edged Atlanta last Sunday. "They're not even in the ball game if our specialty teams do something constructive."

"In this league the best specialty team players only last a year or two," one Redskins player said yesterday. "By that time a guy either gets killed or too smart for the job. It takes a wild breed of man to do the thing right."

"We could use a special team captain here," another Redskin said yesterday. "Maybe he could put some zip into the units. Coach Lombardi might consider it."

Leading candidate for local Captain Who? honors is Dave Kopay, a reckless six-year pro who has been "having fun" throughout his pro career on specialty teams at San Francisco and Detroit.

For the last two games, Kopay and Henry Dyer have been kickoff return men.

"Kopay would be the ideal choice," a teammate said. "He enjoys hitting people, he's got a mean streak and he knows something about these teams. He could give us all a feeling of camaraderie and that's what these teams are about."

The idea fascinated Kopay. "I'd be honored if Coach Lombardi did that," he said. "I enjoy these teams. If you're not playing it's the next best thing. Do the thing right and you don't have to get hurt. I haven't been hurt at it in five years. What you have to do is hit first. If you're reckless, it helps, but you also have to have some football sense."

Sports Log by Earl Luebker: KOPAY AND LOMBARDI. Dave Kopay played his college football under a hard-nosed coach, Jim Owens, at the University of Washington. Things haven't changed a whole lot. Dave's now under Vince Lombardi with the Washington Redskins.

Dave's a veteran of six National Football League seasons and he's lost none of his zest for combat. "I've never been more enthusiastic going into a season," Kopay said. "That's the kind of man Mr. Lombardi is. I'm looking forward to playing fullback for Mr. Lombardi. Whatever Mr. Lombardi does is right although you might not like it at the time.

"I've never been on a team with poorer material than we had at Washington last season," Kopay said, "and Mr. Lombardi got us second-place money in our division."

Kopay is Lombardi's type of football player. All-out is the only way he knows how to play. "I couldn't have been happier when I was traded to Washington. Things had been pretty rough at Detroit, but that's the way it goes."

The Evening Star, Washington, D.C.—Redskins Notes: The tempo was lively and even included an exchange of fisticuffs. Reserve back Dave Kopay took a hard whack from defensive end John Hoffman and squared off. Moments later Kopay was belted by linebacker Marlin McKeever and fired about a dozen punches as McKeever held him off.

In Washington I was able to search about, to drop into bars and restaurants outside the regular nighttime circuits of my teammates. Even so, it was with some teammates that I first visited a bar on Wisconsin Avenue that was a favorite of some gay people. The crowd there was a sufficient mix-up so that nobody even looked up if gays, or football players, walked in.

On the night Bob Long and I went there for a sandwich, he

left me sipping on an Irish coffee and listening to the music. I sat there against the wall, and found myself staring at a nice-looking young man sitting at the bar. I was told later that I always looked like I had a wall around me in those days. I sat there for hours, catching this man's eye several times, but not able to get up the nerve to move toward him.

Finally he got up and left, and I followed him outside. He stopped at the next corner and we chatted. We got into my car and drove to a spot under a freeway ramp near Foggy Bottom. We talked for a while, then ended up hugging and kissing. I was very excited, but I didn't have the vaguest idea what I wanted to do next. I got his telephone number and drove him back to his car.

I put this encounter out of my mind as I got more involved in the football season. Also my parents came for a visit, the first time they had ever been to Washington. They stayed at my house in Georgetown, and we had a really nice time going to the restaurants in the area—-they especially liked Clyde's, where we would sit for hours eating the homemade soups and sipping Irish coffees.

While my parents were visiting I again went to the Wisconsin Avenue bar, and again found the man I had met there. We made plans to meet later, after I had taken my folks out to dinner, and we did meet as planned. We went on to several singles bars, getting as drunk as Ted Robinson and I used to get.

My new friend wasn't at all impressed by my job as a professional football player, which I liked because it meant he wasn't just another fan. We went to a Holiday Inn, and I signed my name "David Marquette." I was very nervous. I even asked for his Army identification card. Except for those frustrating times in college with Ted Robinson, this was the first time I had ever slept with a man. More important, this man was somebody who was up front about his feelings, who knew what he wanted to do and wouldn't lie about it the next morning.

144

I told my parents I stayed with a friend that night. If I had said I was out with a woman they wouldn't have approved of that either. Besides, by then I had learned that each time you tell one lie you trap yourself in another.

I had also been dating Mary Ann Riley since I had come to Washington, and found I still enjoyed being with her, still liked holding her and sleeping with her. We went to team parties and I felt safe as far as outward appearances went, but when we were alone I was still convinced that I wasn't measuring up to the public stud she first started dating—and it bothered me.

One night, when we were naked in bed together, I couldn't help thinking that I really didn't want to be there and kept wondering why the hell I went on trying to please her. In this mood, and reminding myself how easy she had always seemed about sex, I decided to tell her I was homosexual and that that was the reason I couldn't do more for her in bed. I felt it was important for me to let her know that it had nothing to do with her but that I had to be honest with her so she wouldn't go on hoping for something that just wasn't there.

I could hardly believe it when she said it really didn't matter to her at all, that it wouldn't affect our relationship and that—she never stopped saying it—she only wanted to be the only woman in my life.

Maybe a friendship between us could have existed without sex, but it's hard to see how either of us could have expected our relationship to last when Mary Ann wanted to have sex (and I'm convinced she did no matter what she said). It's one thing to be tolerant of someone's occasional fling with another person, something very different to know they actually prefer somebody of a different sex.

And yet Mary Ann and I continued to see each other—maybe partly for reasons as complicated as what happened one night when we met a man in Clyde's who worked as an aide to a conservative Southern congressman and we found ourselves, over drink and talk, getting along so well that Mary Ann and I invited him back to her apartment. After a while, along with more drinks, we ended up in bed together. Without any special pressure to make myself perform with her, I was able to be intimate with Mary Ann at the same time that it was the man who actually excited me. The fact that she seemed turned on by him also helped.

Even before coming to the Redskins I had heard talk about certain players there who were homosexual, but because of my own fears of being discovered I never asked their names and apparently blocked them out if I ever did hear them. The result was I had no idea who they were when I first joined the Redskins.

One was Bill Stiles [fictional name], an all-pro respected by his teammates on the field and personally liked by most of them too. For myself, I admired the way Stiles played and his casual manner with his teammates. He was also a friend of my friend Walter Rock, so it was natural that we would spend some time with each other—we went out drinking and to parties for a long time before I had any idea that he was homosexual. Since at the time I still didn't want to admit to myself that I was homosexual, I also avoided recognizing it in somebody else.

Finally, though, one night at dinner Stiles and I began dropping some clues to each other, and after a while we were able to talk fairly openly about having sex with men.

Stiles and another Redskin took me to a gay bar in Baltimore—none of us would have dared go to one in Washington. We drove all the way to Baltimore to stand around in this hole of a place, an ordinary bar full of ordinary people. I felt let down, except that unlike the time with Maxine Yerby and her friends in Detroit, this time I had gone off purposely looking for a gay situation—in that sense a first and so for me a kind of adventure.

A while later Stiles and I had been to a party, and were so drunk we got lost on our way back to a friend's house outside Washington, where we both were staying. I took off my clothes and fell asleep as soon as I closed my eyes. I woke up with Stiles lying on top of me, kissing me all over. I had never felt anything like this. I was in a kind of ecstasy lying there in the arms of this person I shared so much with. Just holding him, kissing him, was the strongest sexual experience I had known up to that time. But what he wanted to do was fuck me. And that was the word he used. I kept wondering what in hell he was talking about. Incredible as it may sound now, I still didn't accept that this was possible between two men. In my other homosexual encounters the possibility of anal sex had never been mentioned—I hadn't even been able to accept the fantasy. The only kind of anal sex I had ever experienced had been with the go-go dancer in Seattle.

After a while Stiles went back to his bed and I went to sleep. The next morning I woke up remembering how great I had felt with him. I was thinking, hey, I'm not the only one. I always knew there were others but I didn't know that from my own experience. The others, I always figured, were hiding their feelings the way I did. Now I thought I had found a real relationship, I was ready to be lovers for life. I worshipped the man. He rejected me cold. I got into bed with him and he no longer had any interest in holding me. I felt destroyed by his rejection. I couldn't understand why he didn't feel the way I felt toward him. I couldn't believe his feelings had changed so drastically overnight. After that Stiles would never talk about what we had done. Like my college friend Tom he pretended that nothing had ever happened. We were no more than just friends after this, and I stayed depressed by his rejection for a long time. It made me doubt that any kind of lasting happiness was possible for me as a homosexual.

"Bisexual" is a term Stiles and I would use about ourselves at that time. In his anonymous interview for the *Star* series he said he liked having sex with men as much as he did with women. That is a way of putting it, I guess, that's intended to make it more acceptable, maybe even to other football players. The word "bisexual" also fits the swinger's image—and most everybody can go along with that.

As far as I'm concerned, though, these bisexual experiences are more a way of getting two men together than a mutual sharing between a woman and two men. When I was on active Army reserve duty in Texas a college friend and I would share a room—and a prostitute—when we had leave time off the base. What I enjoyed was making it with her after she had been with him. If we hadn't shared her, we wouldn't have had relations with her at all. At the time it was the only acceptable way he and I could be together in a sexual act.

Not long ago I was at a golf tournament in Palm Springs and was talking about bisexuality with an all-pro basketball player who has been married since he was in college. He told me he and his buddy—also an all-pro in the NBA—had made it with a prostitute, and he described the three of them getting in and out of the tub together. "It was really hot," he said.

"Well," I said, "don't you think that's at least a kind of bisexual experience?" "What do you mean?" he said threateningly. I said that even if he weren't directly involved with his friend, didn't he think at least part of what turned him on about the experience had a lot to do with his friend being there. "Yeah," he said, "I guess maybe you're right, probably I wouldn't have wanted to make it with her or with anyone there but him."

People are always asking me now about the "three quarterbacks" in professional football who are supposed to be homosexual. First of all, I would never have limited the number to just three. *The Washington Star* said that, not I. I don't know if there are three or thirty. Stiles once told me about making it with several other players, and more than one has come up to me recently and confided, "I'm just a big closet case myself—but right now I can't deal with it."

What I do know is that I lived a double life all those years and few people inside football and nobody outside ever suspected that I was homosexual, and I was not that different from my teammates.

Everybody associated with the Washington Redskins knows about Stiles' homosexuality, but he refuses to believe this. Apparently being "respected" is so important to him he can't imagine a time when he would risk losing it by talking about his true sexual preference. After my name appeared in the *Star*'s series on homosexuality, Bill Stiles suddenly disappeared from my life. I've seen him only once or twice since and both times by accident. He is not in if I call, he doesn't return calls if I leave a message.

I don't resent Stiles. I resent whatever it is that keeps us from being friends. I pity him for reaching a point of such success in football and still having to live such a fearful life. I hope the time will come when he won't have to be afraid of his own name.

Twenty

THE literature of homosexuality in American sports has been largely confined to subtlety and innuendo. The extraordinary nationwide response to *The Washington Star* series reflects the nearly total absence of writing on the subject.

A major exception is *The Front Runner*, a novel by Patricia Nell Warren, the story of a track coach and a young runner and their love for each other. Both of them have been dismissed at earlier schools because of their homosexuality, both of them have chosen to live openly as homosexual lovers. There is even a marriage at the small college where the lovers found a home. More important to the sports community is the way Warren's characters interact with the sports establishment, which tries to disqualify the young runner before the Olympics. The other athletes at the 1976 Olympics elect the homosexual runner to carry the American flag in the opening parade. He is going for a gold medal and a new world record in the long-distance run when he is killed by an assassin.

The Front Runner was generally ignored by reviewers—except in gay publications—when it was published. Two years later, however, Robert Lipsyte, frequent *New York Times* contributor and author of *Sports World: An American Dreamland*, wrote in a review of another book in *The New York Times*: "*The Front Runner* . . . lifted the genre to a new level by integrating the inevitable win-lose drama with a credible relationship that is both nourished and hampered by sports."

Before *The Front Runner* was published, the two books most people thought of when the subject of homosexuality was mentioned were Dave Meggyesy's *Out of Their League* and Jim Bouton's *Ball Four*. Just the mention of homosexuality in these books seemed to stick in many sports fans' memories. Homosexuality in sports? Oh yeah, Bouton and Dave Meggyesy wrote all about that in their books. In fact, there are only a few words in both books about homosexuality in sports.

Here is the extent of Meggyesy's discussion of homosexuality in professional football: "The sex thing in pro football is strange. One year the word was out around the league that homosexuality was fairly open in one NFL locker room. One veteran of that team told me that those players who were 'in on the program' would stay after practice until all the straights had left and then do their thing. According to this player, about fifteen of his teammates were involved."

Jim Bouton was invited to appear with David Kopay on a television talk show because of his reputation as one who had written on homosexuality in sports. *Ball Four* has these two references only to homosexuality:

"There is often homosexual kidding among the players. Tonight Roy Oyler combed his hair forward and started mincing around the clubhouse, lisping 'hello, sweetheart,' or 'C'mere, you sweet bitch.' Then Gary Bell said, 'Ray, you convinced me. You really are queer.' And Ray said, 'Well, it doesn't make me a bad person.' "

And: "One of our jocko things is to mince around like a fairy, which is pretty funny sometimes, especially while wearing baseball underwear. There is something hilarious about a lumpy, hairy guy trying to act like a queer while wearing the things we wear under a baseball uniform. Take my word."

In *Big Bill Tilden, The Truimphs and the Tragedy*, Frank Deford treats Tilden's homosexuality as "the tragedy." He also writes: "How incredibly difficult it must have been for him: a lifetime in the midst of the most complete, secure heterosexual community. There are virtually no homosexuals in big-time male sports . . . Granted the odd player can get by in any sport living in the closet, but in athletics, in a macho environment, where the players are rooming with one another, running around with one another (often after women), any homosexual would be hard put to conceal his true status for long."

David Kopay was never taken as a homosexual until the last year or so of his career when he started talking about it himself. He had been the official escort of various attractive women while his sexual preference was for men. Wasn't Deford talking about appearances? Does he know the secret thoughts and private actions of professional athletes well enough to say there are virtually no homosexuals among them? The authors put these questions to Deford in writing. He did not answer.

Tom Dowling in *Coach, A Season with Lombardi* says: "I was told that when Paul Hornung and Max McGee were roommates, they used to stage a ritual game of breaking Lombardi's curfew and when Lombardi made the 11 p.m. bed check, he found the pair of them grinning up at him, naked in one another's arms. 'Jesus Christ,' Lombardi is supposed to have said, 'you guys do need a night on the town.' Freudians may gasp but the point is that football players live in a realm that is beyond guilt and the suspicion of sexual ambiguity. 'You've got to be mentally tough,' Lombardi says, and when a football player loses his supreme confidence in his super masculinity, he is in deep trouble."

In the six years since he wrote his book, Dowling's attitudes about homosexuality appear to have expanded if not changed altogether. He now speaks of numerous homosexuals being in professional football and says: "It's no news to any of us that there is a latent homosexual quality to all men to some degree. It is quite clear in athletics that there is a great deal of admiration of the male physique. It's not unlike Socrates sitting around the gymnasium admiring the bodies of the young athletes."

In Dan Jenkins' novel, *Semi-Tough*, the relationship between the two male football players seems the focus of the book. One of them observes: "Some people say Sam might like boys better than girls, and that's why he's never been married, but I hesitate to believe something like this about a friend."

The most explicitly homosexual references in a book about professional football are in the novel *North Dallas Forty*, by Peter Gent, who played split end with the Dallas Cowboys. It is a rarity—a book about sports that was reviewed as literature. Author Larry King praised Gent as a writer who happened to play football, rather than the reverse.

Gent's book includes a kind of contemporary American version of the nude wrestling scene in D. H. Lawrence's *Women in Love*. The scene takes place between Crawford and Claridge, two players who share an apartment and then buy a house together:

"When Crawford straightened up, Claridge pounced and grabbed him by his biceps. Soon they were reeling around in a friendly pushing match, each gripping the other's arms. Laughter and groans punctuated the contest as both men strained mightily against each other. From the color of their faces and the cords standing out on their necks, I could see they were exerting fiercely. Crawford suddenly lost his footing and Claridge stumbled forward on top of him, both of them crashing through the dining room table and chairs. Crawford had ripped off Claridge's shirt, and they lay gasping . . . They were sweating profusely, looking at each other and laughing. Claridge whispered something to Crawford, then carefully held Crawford's face with both hands and planted an open-mouthed kiss full on the lips. Crawford responded and their tongues strained against each other. The embrace lasted about ten seconds."

Later in the book the narrator talks about "a curious, subtle homosexual bond that united the wives in their battles against the husbands and vice versa." He leaves a party where an orgy is taking place because "I'm afraid I'd end up with a guy and like it." Another player calls the narrator a "fuckin' queer." The narrator says that his wife "told the court I was a homosexual. I probably am, nothing would surprise me anymore." At the end of *North Dallas Forty*, the narrator stands facing the coach and owners of the team. He has just been fired for being involved with the fiancée of the owner's brother and he shouts at his accusers: "You got guys on this team screwing each other's wives. And each other—"

In a jacket blurb Dan Jenkins called *North Dallas Forty* "Brutally true."

Apparently in reaction to *The Washington Star* series— since there has been no other journalism on the subject— Michael Novak wrote the following in *The Joy of Sports:*

"Recently, the moralistic impulse has uncovered homosexuality in sports. Muckrakers have informed us that homosexuals appear in professional sports at about the same frequency as elsewhere in our society. Writers used to leer about fanny-patting, celibate training camps, nudity and team showering, and wrestling matches on the soapy floor. The new muckrakers seem to want to give a double message: 'See, the world of sports is corrupt and hollow, a world of fake machismo, infested by gays. But it's all right to be gay, it's great, it's fine.' They want it both ways."

Novak, we suggest, is mistaken in apparently reducing the motives of the *Star* editors and reporter Lynn Rosellini—and of authors such as the authors of this book—to moralistic muckraking. The *Star* and Lynn Rosellini don't need us to defend them. As for ourselves, we're hardly muckrakers; we don't see the world of sports as "infested" by homosexuals. We also don't intend to be special pleaders. We're not uncovering anything that has not been there all along. The only thing new is that more people are now able to talk about it.

Novak concludes the chapter in which he discusses homosexuality: "Assuming one begins with limited hopes, there is more to admire in sports—and in our humanity, and in our nation—than to despise."

We would add that homosexuality is a natural part of sports, as it is of our society and nation. We believe that any kind of human sexuality genuinely felt and honestly expressed is admirable.

Twenty-One

By the end of the 1969 Redskin season I had finally admitted to myself that I was homosexual. I decided I would try to relax and enjoy it and headed for Acapulco for Christmas and New Year's Day.

On the flight I met two college boys and we rented an apartment together, but after two days I had to explain to them that I wanted a place by myself. I also explained why I had come to Acapulco, which didn't involve going out looking for women as we had been doing.

I went to an elaborate men's boutique, bought myself the first pairs of flared pants I had ever owned, the first sandals I had ever worn, the first bright-colored shirts I had ever dared to put on.

Every day I would run on the beach in the intense tropical sun, feeling free and good. One afternoon I was resting after a run and saw an attractive young man looking at me. He came over and invited me to join his friends on Paradise Beach for a drink. I was nervous and reluctant, but I went.

This was when I met a lively middle-aged man who owned a chain of stores back in the States. The group also included the owner of one of the largest construction companies in the midwest and two or three others of similar wealth. The store owner lived near a university, was a major supporter of the football team and frequently gave parties for the players and their dates—his only requirement being that they swim naked in his pool.

I went along to dinner with him that night, and looked at his pictures and listened to his stories of the football players. Later I was to learn that a professional football teammate had been to that university and had taken part in the parties the older man described.

When I mentioned that I was looking for a job, the man immediately suggested I talk with a friend of his who was a very successful businessman in the northeast. Actually I had already taken an off-season job with a large company near Washington, but after several days in the plant I realized that I would be going into a situation that was suspicious at best. The owner of the company—who had a wife and children— had just hired another athletic-looking young man. The other employees were openly resentful of the favors shown that newcomer—especially when word got around that he accompanied the owner on hunting and fishing trips to South America and other places. I, too, was invited to go along on these trips.

One morning I got a call in Acapulco from the business executive the store owner had mentioned. He convinced me that I should join his firm as an assistant to the president. I had no idea then how this decision was eventually going to affect me. Of course I had apprehensions, but it all seemed so smooth and easy I wasn't thinking about the psychological consequences. Besides, most of the ballplayers I knew had used connections made in sports to join some business at the top. Sometimes these connections were made through girl friends or wives, sometimes through the businessmen who hung around the locker room or showed up at parties and bars where the players went. More than a few ballplayers I had known actually bragged about the "sugar daddies" who kept them on retainers in exchange for an occasional blow job. Two or three of my Redskin teammates eventually knew about my new junior executive position and said they thought it was great—no matter what conditions were attached to it.

I flew into the city where Brad Furman's [fictional name] offices were located. The plan was to meet him for breakfast the next morning, but he arrived an hour early, while I was still shaving. Later he told me he saw me standing there in my

157

Jockey shorts with a fresh Acapulco tan and fell in love on sight. There were times when I loved being with the man, but I was never in love with him. I was never even attracted to him sexually. He was middle-aged, short and overweight, married with children. But that first morning I think I was flattered by his instant approval and affection. It also puffed me up some to be important to a man who wielded so much power and influence.

It was understood from the beginning that I would be expected to provide certain sexual favors in return for the job. I told him he could go down on me, but there was no possibility I would ever feel enough to respond the same way to him. That was fine with him. At first I was easily aroused—it was a completely new experience—and in the newness I didn't sense how degrading this exercise would become to me.

Furman took stock of my clothes, said those flared pants wouldn't do in his business world, and bought me three expensively tailored conservative suits. He helped me find a good apartment in a luxury high-rise building, but I insisted on paying the rent and furnishing it. We shopped for a stereo and he bought an elaborate model labeled "no limitations worth mentioning." "That's you," he said. He kept wanting to buy things for me, and I told him more and more that I didn't want his gifts.

I was introduced to everybody in his office as a man from "Vince Lombardi's Redskins who is here to learn the business." It was important to Furman that Lombardi had traded for me. He had seen the film Lombardi and Jerry Kramer did for businessmen and he was always quoting lines the coach had said. In fact Furman saw himself as a sort of Lombardi of the business world. Like Lombardi, he was an absolute ruler and saw the rest of America revolving around his "empire," a word he used a lot. When he would pull off an unusually profitable deal he would describe it to me, smile and say, "I'm a number one draft choice."

I was paranoid from the start about what his people were

thinking about me. I asked Furman what I should say if anybody in the office asked how we met. He said nobody would say a word "because they'll accept my decision as to whom I hire. I hired them and I can fire them."

Regardless of how I got there, at the beginning I was serious about learning the business, and self-conscious that I was automatically welcomed as a knowledgeable businessman because I was a member of Vince Lombardi's Redskins. But the more I stayed there, the more I realized that there was no real job for me. I wasn't learning anything and I knew I didn't belong there.

We went to various restaurants and talked football constantly. His partners were left with the impression that I was a young stud out procuring girls for the boss. This kind of talk only made me feel more like a fool. "Boy, you should have seen this gal the other day," Furman would lie, "she wanted to put the make on him right there."

The only thing that kept me going was the thought of going back to football in June. I hated the conservative suits and being indoors all day. I was actually frightened of going into the office every day, wondering how I would look busy and fill up my hours. I knew I would never get the same excitement or satisfaction out of making money that Furman did. My whole life had involved a healthy coordination of body and mind on the playing field, where I could let my emotions flow naturally through my body. For me, professional football was the ideal situation of being paid for this absolute physical exertion I enjoyed more than anything else.

One of Furman's best friends was a powerful lawyer whose every other sentence to me was "faggot this" or "queer that." And yet when he met me it was, "Oh, wow, I'm really glad you're here. You seem to have more smarts than the other jocks. Most of them are happy working at car dealerships." I was thinking—what's so wrong with car dealerships?

We would be at lunch and the lawyer would be talking like a schoolboy about some tough linebacker he admired. The next sentence would be a crack about the nelly waiter. Then he would invite me out to swim with him or play tennis or spend a day at his golf club. There were never any women with us.

Most of the men that I've met like this lawyer seem to be able to talk of almost nothing but getting away from their wives and children. Furman, however, was actually a considerate and, so far as I could tell, even a loving family man, and there was no question that they came first in his life. He saw me only during the day. Nights and weekends he went home.

Seeing his relationship with them made me think that it might be possible for a homosexual man to have a happy family life—just as possible as it seems to be for some heterosexual men to have families and still see other women. Furman had heard me talk about my stewardess friend, and he kept encouraging me to get married. He just couldn't believe, though, that Mary Ann Riley actually knew about my homosexuality and still loved me. He believed that it would be the end of his family life and business career if it were known that he was homosexual. I didn't—and don't—believe that.

I do know that the whole absurdity of having to lie, having to hide, helped to cheapen the experience and erode my self-respect. As the weeks wore on, I thought less and less of myself for taking a job under those conditions. Nearly every morning before work Furman would arrive at my apartment. I came to resent him bitterly and was revolted by the act I was letting myself participate in.

When I finally left to go back to training camp I knew I was never coming back, but for months after this Furman would call me wherever I was. He came to visit me once in Washington, and during that visit I made it clear to him that whatever relationship we had had was finished. He cried uncontrollably as I drove him to the airport that last time. He looked like an emotional wreck at that moment, but I also was aware that he still had the love of his wife and children, even if they couldn't provide everything he needed and wanted.

As I got further away from the experience with Furman I really began to feel deeply depressed about it—although for the first few weeks of camp I was too involved in practice to think much of anything else, and there was also an incident there that on the one hand terrified me but also made me think it just might be possible to live more openly as a homosexual with at least some of my teammates.

The incident involved John Jaqua—a handsome young rookie the sportswriters described as if they too were infatuated by him. He was an aggressive defensive back. An outgoing, friendly guy, he was one of the most popular men on the team. During the rookie entertainment periods Jaqua would sing, "Wanderin' Star" with a gusto I can still recall, and the other players would be moved to join in singing with him.

Jaqua had grown up on a ranch in Oregon. He was a rugged man, but his features and his build were so finely drawn he looked like a Greek statue come to life. Bill Stiles was so taken with him he would stay after practice every day and work with him to help him make the team. I kept encouraging Jaqua as John Brodie had encouraged me when I started out in San Francisco, and after a while he started believing me when I said he was going to make it.

One night after one of the pre-season exhibition games Bill Stiles and I got very drunk. We went to a gay discotheque, I think we were so drunk we even danced together. We went back to our hotel, and I assumed Stiles was going to sack out in the other bed in my room. The next morning I woke up to see the bed was in a mess, all of Stiles' clothes were there, he was nowhere in sight.

I was having breakfast with three other players when Jaqua came up, looking pale and frightened. He asked if he could talk with me. We walked into the lobby where we could be alone. He said Stiles had come to his room the night before and asked if he could sleep there because he had lost the keys to his own room. Jaqua's roommate was asleep in the other bed.

Jaqua said Stiles was trying to hug and kiss him, so he pulled him into the bathroom to talk. And then Stiles started crossing himself and saying, "God forgive me, I don't know what I'm doing . . ."

"That was really crazy, Dave. What should I do?" I didn't condemn or defend Stiles because I knew I could have done the same thing. Instead I told him that obviously Stiles cared a lot about him and that he had also shown he had a lot of respect for Stiles.

Sitting together on the bus back to camp I was really nervous. Finally Jaqua asked, "I wonder where his head is?" and I said something like, "Nobody knows where anybody's head is." But I was really thinking mostly about my own. It did impress me, though, that Jaqua was trying to be understanding about what happened to him with Stiles, and that afterward he didn't mention it to anyone else and they stayed friends.

As the year wore on, however, I was feeling more and more depressed. I was unhappy with my performance on the field, and my sexual anxiety only got worse as I thought more about the time I had spent with the business executive.

One night I met John Jaqua for drinks at Clyde's in Georgetown and we talked about my depression. I asked him about a doctor in Los Angeles he had mentioned to me, an analyst and hypnotist named William J. Bryan, Jr. John said the doctor had helped him overcome the constant pain he felt when he started playing ball. Maybe he could help me out of my depression.

It was a gloomy wet day and I was thinking that maybe this was the time—since I had helped him after the incident with Stiles—I could level with Jaqua about my own homosexuality. I had driven him out to his girl friend's, and we were parked, talking, in front of her apartment building. I told him I was a homosexual. He said, "That's amazing." Then he said he had to be going. I was really frightened. My first thought was that John would tell everybody else. "John, I'm sharing this with you, this is something for you to know," and then I quoted Lombardi's line: "What you say here, what you see here, what you hear here, let it stay here when you leave here." John said, "No problem," and quickly got out of the car.

He had said "no problem," but we were never again close after that. Ironically, he and Stiles remained close friends—I assume because they pretended their encounter never happened. Stiles only shrugged it off when I asked him about it.

The one person I could relate to during this time was not one of my teammates but one of their wives—Betty Ann Rock, who was wonderfully warm and understanding. She wasn't shocked by anything I told her. She understood, without condemning, how and why I could be so depressed about that so-called junior executive position.

My second season in Washington, I wasn't playing much, which gave me more unwanted time to brood about my personal feelings. Coach Lombardi was in the hospital dying, and that seemed to weigh heavy on me too. I kept thinking of something he had said: "The quality of one's life is in direct proportion to one's commitment to excellence." I told myself I didn't have this integrity he talked about—in football, yes, but not in my private life.

The last time most of us saw Lombardi was during a practice at Georgetown University we called during the Players Association strike. Sonny Jurgensen was calling the drills when we saw this big black limousine pull onto the edge of the field. Somehow we all knew who it was and we knew he wasn't able to come charging out toward us the way he always had before.

Somebody helped him out of the car, and he just stood there while we gathered around him. There was none of the bark left in his voice. He just talked quietly as each one of us came up to shake his hand. He had come to say good-bye. He knew it. We knew it. Later, at the funeral in St. Patrick's

Cathedral in New York, we sat as a team while The Coach was eulogized.

Like the voice of God, Lombardi's memory came back to haunt me in my depression. I was weak. I had sold out by taking that job with Furman. I was not mentally tough. I read newspaper stories about a mass murderer in Northern California. Was I that crazy? I had been crazy enough to get myself into that awful position with Furman. I had to do something but I had no idea which way to turn—except toward home and my family.

As I flew back to Los Angeles I never felt more alone. I was so choked up I really thought I was losing control of myself. My brother Tony met me at the airport, and I broke down as we were driving back to my parents' house. I told him I had never been so depressed, that sometimes I thought I was losing control of my mind. Tears were coming down my cheeks. Tony, clearly, was affected. He tried to reassure me. "You can handle it, everything's going to be okay." Later that night I asked Tony to come into the back bedroom where we could talk. I told him bluntly that I was homosexual. It didn't seem to be a problem with him. He could see how disturbed I was, and I felt he was showing that he was honestly concerned about me. Later his reaction would seem to contradict this, but I think that was because he had to deal with it publicly—this was very similar to my dad's reaction too.

My mother couldn't understand what I was doing home, why wasn't I back at my terrific executive's position with Furman's company? I told her I had had a very difficult year, that I was very depressed. This must have been hard for my parents to understand—after all, I had been successful enough to buy them a new car.

Not long after I got back to Los Angeles I called Dr. William J. Bryan, Jr., and made an appointment. Just admitting that I needed professional help was a tremendous step for me. I kept reminding myself that John Jaqua had gone to the same doctor and there was nothing strange about him—he was a very together guy who got along well with the ladies.

On a football team if you have something wrong with you you go to a doctor. He fixes it and your body takes over and heals it for you. I thought it would be the same with this problem in my head. I thought Bryan would just fix me up, and that my head would heal the same way a torn hamstring does.

Twenty-Two

THE doctor's office was on the fourth floor of an ordinary office building on Sunset Strip. I walked down a narrow hallway lined with pictures of the doctor and his famous clients. Turning into the office, I was confronted by an amazing looking man. He was huge (more than 300 pounds) and slovenly looking. In some other setting he would have been revolting to me, but his life was separate from my world, and there were all these college degrees staring at me. If they could help, I didn't care what he looked like.

The makings of a chicken sandwich were dribbling onto Bryan's thick red beard as he ate and talked, sounding as though he were giving a speech. He said he sometimes felt he was the reincarnation of the first William Jennings Bryan, his first cousin twice removed. He said he had treated more than 15,000 patients, more than Freud and Mesmer combined. He said he had just had most of his intestines removed in order to lose weight and that he had gone through the operation under self-induced hypnosis and without anesthesia. Well, if he could do all that, I was thinking, maybe he could help me.

Bryan asked me what my problem was. I told him I was very depressed. He asked why. I said I was homosexual and that had gotten me into some very confusing situations.

"Well," Bryan said with a chuckle, "I'm going to tell you right now there's no way you are a homosexual." "I definitely am," I said. I had come to be cured of my depression, not my homosexuality, although the two were surely related. I realize it might seem to some people that this depression of mine had a lot of self-pity in it—and maybe they would be right. I was certainly feeling very alone, as though I, David Kopay, was the only one who had ever suffered through times of such painful confusion.

"Well, sit back in your chair," Bryan was saying now. "No problem. We can cure this in no time at all." The fee was to be $1,500, but there was no mention of how many sessions it would take to cure me. I said okay. I was desperate enough to try anything. I thought I would just sit back and let him cure me—I didn't realize I was going to have to do it myself.

We went back to the hypnosis room, which looked more like a tacky hotel room—windows blacked out with tinfoil, a plain white table, a reclining massage chair. Bryan was talking the whole time, his voice loud and powerful, explaining that some people accept hypnosis readily and others resist it. I kept reminding myself that Jaqua must have gone through the same thing, so I did as Bryan told me, laid my head back and put my feet up. Bryan then flipped on a switch and the chair started to vibrate.

I was thinking how silly it was, and I started smiling until Bryan came up and closed my eyelids with his hand. I decided to give it a chance. "Deeper and deeper on down," he said. "Relax. Relax. Deeper and deeper on down."

I gave in to it. I let myself relax in a way I never had before. "Your only concern is to relax," he said. "Nothing will bother you. Nothing affects you. You feel very comfortable as you go deeper and deeper on down. You feel very, very relaxed. You're going deeper and deeper on down . . ."

After a while he said, "David, I'm just going to put these earphones on you and you're going to relax and listen to the tape and feel very comfortable. Nothing bothers you."

A nurse came in and adjusted the earphones. The tape started playing soft classical music that would fade in and out as the doctor's voice came on. "You're at the beach," he would say, "feel the warmth of the sun. Feel the breeze. Smell the air. Hear the sea gulls." And I could hear the sea gulls and the waves, the sounds refreshing my mind with pleasant memories.

The tape finished, and the nurse told me the session was over. I remember walking out into the sunshine asking myself what I had done. I went off to the beach and thought, well, this is really it, why was I paying to hear a tape recording of it?

After the first session I saw very little of the doctor. He would ask me how I was doing, I would tell him I was still full of fears, still depressed. He would insist I was heterosexual. I would tell him, "Listen, doctor, I know I am turned on by men," and he would say, "I know, you told me that before. But women are very attracted to you. Hell, every one of my women in this place would like to screw you. You are a heterosexual."

For several weeks I just saw one of Bryan's assistants and listened to the tapes. Finally I demanded to have personal sessions with the doctor himself. He told me I would have a dream and I would come back and discuss it with him. And that night I dreamt about my parents being on an airplane. I remember the plane breaking up and crashing into the ocean. I swam away from it toward safety. I felt good that I had survived but guilty about what had happened to them. I woke up crying, shocked that I could have such a dream—which I now think meant that I wanted to escape, break loose from the old beliefs and fears they had raised me with. And breaking loose was a scary and guilt-making process.

Bryan thought differently. "Obviously," he said, "the dream symbolized an attempt to kill your heterosexuality. Your parents were heterosexual and they were killed. But you don't want your folks killed, and you don't want your heterosexuality killed."

When I told my parents I was seeing an analyst, my mother was shocked. She said there was nothing wrong with me, all I needed to do was to go to church and pray. It was then I decided to tell my parents I was homosexual. I asked them to come into the living room and sit down. I said I loved them very much. I said I could not pretend any longer. I wanted them to accept and love me for everything I really was.

"You keep asking me why I'm going to an analyst. Well, I've been very depressed, and I've told you that. I'm trying to figure out why I'm so depressed and so fearful of everything. Look," I finally said, "I'm a homosexual."

My mother sat there, stunned. "David, you are not a homosexual." I said, "Mother, I know I am." Dad seemed very calm about it, just like Tony at first. "Well," he said, "there's nothing I can do about it now."

Mother then became hysterical. She yelled at me, "Why do you feel this way? Why are you saying this? Are you blaming this on me?" I said, "I'm not blaming anybody, Mother. It's a fact." She asked if Mary Ann Riley knew. I said she did. She asked if my other friends knew. I said they did.

"Look," I said, crying myself by then, "sometimes there are no explanations." Mother was screaming, "You're not, you're not . . . David, when did this happen? . . . when you went away to school?" I told her I had been a homosexual for a long time, that homosexuality wasn't uncommon among professional ball players. She asked about Ted Robinson. I told her he and I had slept together. "I hope he burns in hell," she said. I told her that was a horrible thing to say. "He made you a homosexual." "No, he definitely did not make me a homosexual."

"I created you and I can destroy you," she said, and then I grabbed her and we just held each other for a long time, with her sobbing, "No, no, no . . ." As I was leaving she said, "I never want to see you again." I turned to my father. "How do you feel?" "You heard what your mother said."

That was one of the rare times I had ever heard my parents supporting each other in anything—and I was thinking that even then. I ran out of the house and was getting into the car when Dad stopped me. "I didn't really mean that," he said. "Your mother didn't mean it either. I had to say that for her sake." "I know, Dad, I understand."

There was nobody I could go to then, nobody except Dr. William J. Bryan, Jr. In our sessions he asked me about my childhood, and I told him about a time when I got hit in the head with a baseball bat and my mother took a large steel knife and put it on ice. Of course she was only preparing it to lay against my head to offset swelling, but I thought she was going to cut the knot off. "You see," Bryan said, "you thought she was going to cut something else off."

I laughed at that. But at least the process of being forced to look inside myself more was helping me to examine my homosexuality in ways I never had before. I just wasn't coming up with the doctor's conclusions. The more he tried to convince me I was heterosexual, the more I accepted that I was mainly homosexual.

While I was in this process of coming to terms with my homosexuality, it also seemed important for me to know that I could still make it with a woman. I didn't want my preferring sex with men to keep me from having relations with women. In fact, I felt that if I were truly at ease with my homosexuality, then I should be able to go ahead with a normal relationship with Mary Ann. I told Bryan about her and he encouraged the relationship, had me call her from his office. "David obviously cares for you," he told her. "We've talked about you several times." I invited her out for a visit, and not just because Bryan encouraged it but because she was still the only person who knew my whole story and still said she loved me. In spite of the sexual tension that always came between us, I still loved her as a friend. Bryan was convinced it was just a healthy heterosexual relationship that would straighten me out.

When Mary Ann arrived I was determined to go through with sex with her, and feeling especially anxious about it. I was doing it to prove a point, not because I wanted to or felt

170

any real sexual attraction for her. I just was not naturally aroused by her. I couldn't keep an erection and I blamed her for putting me in this impossible situation. I was shaking her and yelling as if she were to blame for all of my problems. "David," she said, "it's all right. Calm down." And I finally did. We talked about my sessions with Bryan, and she was calm and understanding about these too. She said it made her feel good that I called on her when I was in trouble—after all, that meant she was number one in my life.

Later, under hypnosis, Bryan told me I was now fully capable of handling myself and I should get married to Mary Ann Riley. My response was that I really did care for her, that I felt safe in public because I was more acceptable to my teammates when I had a woman with me, that in private I knew she knew about my homosexuality and didn't care, that I was closer to her than anybody I knew, my folks liked her—okay, why not get married? I came out of hypnosis, and called her.

She said she would be right out, and we would fly to Las Vegas the next day. Bryan agreed to stand as best man. I paid his way to the wedding and back and never saw him again. By this time I had decided I had gotten everything out of his treatment I was going to get. Besides, he kept telling me I was capable of handling myself.

I also called Greg Modesti, my best friend from the Army reserve. I had first told Greg about my homosexuality when we were driving back from a weekend reserve meeting in Apple Valley. I remember how he had swerved off the road and nearly wrecked the car, but we talked about it and it never affected our friendship. He too had always said that Mary Ann was "exactly what you need." He shouted into the phone when I told him I was getting married. "That's fabulous, Dave, I'll meet you in Vegas."

Mary Ann, the doctor and I flew to Las Vegas, got a license and went through the ceremony in a rented chapel. It was unlike any wedding I had ever been to, and I apologized to Mary Ann for that. That day we also had some very frank talk about

171

the whole business. I think we both had doubts about whether our marriage would work, but we decided we would give it a try and if it didn't work we would just get out of it without any hassles.

Greg and his date arrived just after the ceremony and we all went down to the hotel theater, where Little Richard was staging one of his outrageous performances. Everybody was laughing about his costumes and even I was joining in the jokes about being gay.

Mary Ann had to fly back to work, but we met the next week at a summer place her parents owned in northern Michigan. The family could see how anxious and uncomfortable I was in my new role, that I really didn't feel right being there with her or with them. They could see but they couldn't understand.

Our sex life wasn't satisfying to either of us, but we kept trying. We rented a nice apartment in Washington and began furnishing it during the two weeks before I had to leave for training camp with the Redskins—which meant a two-month enforced separation.

During this time I had heard that Ted Robinson was back from Vietnam and was living somewhere in Washington, and one night I called him and invited him by for dinner, thinking now we could just be friends.

After dinner we went to the Hawk and Dove, one of my favorite bars on Capitol Hill. Ted liked being with a Redskin, and I introduced him to everybody in the bar.

Then I told him there was another place I wanted to take him. He followed me in his car, and I led him down to the southwest part of town to one of the largest gay discotheques in Washington, the Pier Nine. By then it was late and the place was jammed with people—mostly men—dancing and laughing.

Ted stood there dumbfounded. He stared at the mass of gay people around us and then turned to me. "What the hell are you doing taking me to a place like this?" "Ted, this is who I am. I'm gay." He just looked at me. "You've known that for a hell of a long time—or you should have. What do you think we were doing all those times we went to bed together? What do you think that was all about?" Ted shot back at me, "I don't know what you're talking about, I never did any of that." I felt disgusted, and was relieved when he said he had to go. That was the last time I ever saw him. Later I heard that he had gone back to Vietnam.

By the summer of my third year in Washington I was going fairly regularly to various gay places of entertainment—and many of my teammates knew it. My close friend Walter Rock—blond, blue-eyed, six feet four, 250 pounds, an offensive tackle who had played for San Francisco when I did—had known for a long time, as did his wife, that I was gay. As a matter of fact, one night he had dinner with Furman and myself and even saw nothing wrong with that relationship.

Several other teammates knew about my homosexuality. One day in the locker room Larry Brown told me his girl friend had seen me at the Pier Nine. The black players—Roy Jefferson, Jim Snowden, Henry Dyer, Charlie Harraway—all knew I was gay and none of them cared one way or the other. It seemed to make for a kind of unspoken bond between us. I knew they had been harassed just because of the color of their skin, and they knew that my difference was also something to be accepted for what it was—not what other people might think it is.

In the locker room we all talked about what condition our bodies were in, but this was athlete's talk and I strongly doubt that anybody who knew about my homosexuality was ever uneasy about me there. People who talk about how uncomfortably tempted a homosexual must be in a locker room full of naked men aren't being sensible. A homosexual has as much control over his sex drives as anybody else, and he especially is aware that the locker room is not the appropriate place for sex. Some people also assume that a homosexual wants any man he sees. That's no more true for homosexuals than it is for heterosexual men surrounded by women. There are some who excite you, and there are many others who don't.

Ironically, while Mary Ann's apparent tolerance and understanding about my preference for men had much to do with my marrying her, it also finally helped bring about the failure of our marriage. True, even after our marriage she never objected to my going to gay bars, never complained that I wasn't more attentive to her needs. And there certainly were qualities about her that I liked and appreciated—she was independent, thrifty, practical. But our sex life, during the infrequent times when we had any, amounted to nothing much more than Mary Ann watching and helping me masturbate, and kissing and hugging each other. She never put any pressure on me to change. When we would talk about it I would tell her, "You're not going to change me," and she would answer, "I don't want to change you." I honestly believe, though, that she did, that the truth was that she wanted me to love and to make love to her—and I didn't, not in the way she really wanted. That was something I couldn't change. We even tried a sexual encounter that I suppose might be considered a try at some kind of compromise. It happened after a night out when we brought back to our apartment a gay friend I had had sex with. Tall, blond, handsome, he was the actual prototype for John Reid's lover in *The Best Little Boy in the World*. He had never had sex with a woman, and yet once we were in bed, before I knew what was happening, he and Mary Ann were so involved with each other I was left out completely.

I got out of the bed and out of the room, angry and frustrated over the contradictions in my head. I was ending up jealous of both of them—of him for being more taken with Mary Ann than me, and of her for giving him all her attention. I didn't want—or wasn't able—to satisfy her myself, and yet I didn't want anybody else to have her. It was an impossible situation, and it forced me to admit what I already knew—that our marriage was all wrong, and would never work.

Mary Ann, though, still didn't want a divorce. The failure of our marriage, for her, was a deeply personal failure, and divorce would be a public acknowledgment of it. But whatever compromises she seemed willing to make, I didn't feel they gave us enough to keep a marriage going. I knew she wanted and needed a more personal commitment that involved sex. I knew, because I wanted and needed the same thing for myself.

It would be several weeks before we actually separated, meanwhile I was doing very well during most of training camp, right up until two weeks before the start of the season when I injured my ankle. The doctor told the coach it wasn't too bad and I should be able to play, but I knew better. I didn't get back into action until the last exhibition game against the Baltimore Colts, who had won the Super Bowl the year before. We lost 20-13, but I scored both touchdowns for the Redskins and felt good about it.

I felt even better at the team party that night when Coach George Allen congratulated me on the game and told me he wanted to give me plenty of playing time from there on in to get ready for the regular season. We had practice on Monday. When the last cuts were made on Tuesday I was officially on the roster. Then on Wednesday one of Allen's assistants called me in and asked for my playbook—I had been cut.

I went in to talk with Allen. He said he had changed his mind at the last minute. There were tears in my eyes. I was trying not to cry openly, trying to keep control. As I walked out of his office I was wishing that this once I had let myself go enough to beat the shit out of him for lying to me. I learned later that Allen had had my replacement in a Washington hotel room for those two weeks when I thought I had made the team.

The Sunday Star—Washington D.C., Sept. 19, 1971, Steve Guback column: THE UNKINDEST CUT. Dave Kopay's voice the other day was very low as if he still were trying to recover from the shock: "I played, I did my job and all of a sudden, nothing."

That was his epitaph. At 29, Kopay suffered the cruelest cut of them all. It had been cut-down week in the National Football League and the landscape is littered now with the broken dreams of Alex Karras, Tom Dempsey, Nick Eddy and, yes, Dave Kopay.

On Tuesday when the 40-man Redskin roster came out, Kopay was on it. He had an inner glow of satisfaction. "Coach Lombardi used to say that people earned their jobs," said Kopay. "I earned my way." The next day Kopay was waived.

"I just can't understand it," the puzzled Kopay said. "I don't know what I can do. I thought I had made the squad."

For two days Kopay refused phone calls. He wanted to think this thing out. Then the reality hit. He has nowhere to go now.

"It's too late," he said, simply. "Every team has its 40-man roster and taxi squad. Yet I know I did my job and played well this season. I don't know what kind of a deal I got."

Yesterday Kopay went to the Redskins office to pick up his final paycheck. The irony of it is that because he made the 40-man team, the Redskins must pay him for the first league game, the one in which he'll never play. That's not important now to Kopay. Kopay wrestled with words and thoughts and there was no answer.

"I had the desire and love for the game, the things Coach Lombardi brought out. That's what he used to say the game was all about. Now it's over. Discarded. That's what hurts.

"I guess this was mostly Allen's decision about me, but I'm disappointed that Ted Marchibroda (backfield coach) didn't stand up more for me. I had my ankle torn up in training camp, but they needed players and I played. I played against

Baltimore and Miami and did well. I thought I played well against Cincinnati. Nobody could have found fault with that."

Indeed, Kopay's statistics were some of the best on the team. He carried 22 times for a 3.2 average, second best to Larry Brown among the regular rushers, and caught eight passes, as many or more than any running back.

Kopay doesn't know what to think anymore. He figured he earned a job, and then lost it. Some cuts never heal, even with the passage of time. Put Dave Kopay in that category.

Mary Ann was very patient with me during this time after I was cut. For days I would break down and cry. I was bitter at Allen and the whole football establishment that had now dumped me. No, I don't think my being cut had anything to do with my being homosexual because I don't think Allen or any of the other coaches knew about it. Besides, they knew about Bill Stiles' homosexuality.

The weekend after I was cut Mary Ann and I went to New York. I told myself the reason for the trip was to see an old friend, a young man I had had sex with. I thought it would be some kind of comfort to see him, but I found him living in a situation I considered even worse than my old arrangement with the businessman.

And I knew the reason I had gone to New York had very little to do with him. The Redskins were playing their first game against the Giants that weekend. It was a game I was being paid to play in and a game I should have been playing in. Like a homing pigeon, I went to Yankee Stadium even though there was no place for me except as another fan up in the stands. I sat there with Mary Ann, but I never felt more alone. I wanted to see Coach Allen humiliated, but I could never cheer against my old friends and teammates. I sat there watching the Redskins kick the hell out of the Giants—and I cried like a baby.

Later that week I got a call from the New Orleans Saints

asking me to sign on with them. I took the next plane and plunged back into the game with the same old spirit of the young rookie that John Brodie had called "Psyche." I left Mary Ann in Washington, and although she visited me once or twice there was never any serious thought of her moving to New Orleans with me. Instead I got a small apartment—an old slave quarter remodeled as an apartment—in the French Quarter, not knowing the area was "off limits" to the team. One of my close friends and neighbors there was a painter named George Dreaux. One day he did a nude charcoal sketch of me. Later I was passing by his studio and saw myself displayed in his show window. I slammed the brakes on in the car and ran into his studio, yelling at him for trying to expose me, trying to ruin my career. He shook his head, led me to the window and showed me that actually what he was doing was holding the drawing up to the light so he could trace a heavier copy of it. Embarrassed, I apologized for what I had said. At the time it seemed a minor incident, but actually I think it was important, another moment to make me aware of the foolishness of hiding my true identity. Afterward I let myself enjoy living among gay friends for the first time.

The Evening Star—Washington, D.C., Oct. 18, 1971: Dave Kopay, bitter after being the last player cut by the Redskins this season, unwittingly made a major contribution to Washington's big gain over Dallas in the National Conference's East Division race.

Kopay was very valuable to the Redskins yesterday—as a specialty team member of the New Orleans Saints. Dallas had scored twice in the second half at New Orleans to close within three points of the Saints and were about to gain possession for probably the last time when Kopay made his appearance. Playing his first game for the Saints, Kopay raced down under a punt and, when the Cowboy's Cliff Harris fumbled it, Kopay recovered on the Dallas three-yard line. Three plays later, Archie Manning scored from the one to seal Dallas' doom.

States-Item, New Orleans—Oct. 20, 1971: Dave Kopay isn't exactly a candidate for Medicare but when you're 29 years old and a member of the New Orleans Saints, you've got to feel a little creaky. Kopay has served on special teams most of his career and enjoys his work. He realizes the importance of the "suicide squad" and the role it plays in the game.

"Special teams contribute about 30 per cent of the action," he says. "It's a very physical job. You look at what the special teams did Sunday against the Cowboys and you'll see how important its work is. It won the game."

After that season in New Orleans I went back to Mary Ann and the apartment in Washington, but in spite of my still liking her and even being grateful to her for the support she had given me after Allen had cut me, the relationship was no more satisfactory. If anything I felt it was worse, and that no matter how much we could do for each other in some ways, I just wasn't capable of the deeper emotional commitment with her I felt I could have with another man. I wanted out, I needed out, but every time I would try to talk with her about leaving she would become hysterical.

Finally, when I told her I was definitely leaving, she said she would slit her wrists. She was actually running to jump off the balcony when I grabbed her and held her back inside the apartment. Through it all she kept saying, "What will my parents think? I'm a failure, I'm a failure." She really had hoped to change me. She had known about my homosexuality from the start. She had known we had trouble relating to each other sexually. And yet she must have felt we could overcome all this and live like a storybook couple in a mythical romance.

I don't think it was Mary Ann's failure, or mine. I'm not even sure "failure" is the right word. But if it is, I think it applies as much to the society that helped push us into roles neither of us naturally fitted.

I did stay with Mary Ann until she calmed down, and then moved in with a friend from the Redskins. I left her our wedding gifts, the furniture, paid a few months advanced rent, and later gave her money to see a psychiatrist. I didn't know what else to do for her. I did know I could no longer go on trying to change into the husband she wanted and needed.

Mary Ann Kopay works now in an office in a large city in the Northeast. She says she likes living there, keeping up with the latest movies and plays.

She also liked her interviewer's choice of a restaurant, the Tout Va Bien. She would meet for a chat but she did not want her side of the story included in the book. "It's David's book," she said. He was a closed chapter in her life. She asked only that her name be changed. Her real name is not "Mary Ann," and "Riley" was not her surname before marriage.

"You know," she said, "you are talking about a very short period of time. I once counted up the days we lived together and do you know how many it was? Forty-five. That's not much time." It seemed that she was straining to be indifferent. It's not necessarily the time involved but the intensity of feeling, her interviewer suggested. "I think all the intensity was on my side," she said.

She had not changed her last name, she said, because she didn't have the money to pay for the legal fees involved. In fact, there is no charge for the process. She could simply revert to her own family name—as did Kopay's sister Marguerite. Perhaps her keeping his name was one more way for her to hold onto Kopay. And the apparent need isn't all one-sided. Kopay himself was still so upset over the memory of their "failed" marriage that he thought it best that he not meet with her during this interview. Even without children or property to settle, the two have still not arranged a legal divorce—five years after they separated.

"All that's over now," said Mary Ann Kopay. "I have friends who don't know I was ever married." What about people in her office? Didn't they connect her name to all the stories about Kopay's homosexuality? Absolutely not, she said. "Nobody in my office knows I was married to him. Nobody has said a word." Did it occur to her that these people were just being polite? No, it had not.

She could once talk tactics and statistics with the best of football players, but now Mary Ann Kopay says she regards professional football as a brutal, dehumanizing sport that has damaged a lot of good people's lives and is really just a business operation for selling television advertising.

But, her interviewer reminded her, she spent several years of her life around professional football players. Kopay was not the only one she had dated. "Yes." She smiled. "I did that. But that's a thing you do as an adolescent, going after the athletes. I'm over all that now."

Twenty-Three

OAKLAND TRIBUNE, July 13, 1972: WISER KOPAY RETURNS. Dave Kopay drove back into the Bay area yesterday on his way to the Oakland Raiders' training camp, memories filtering through his mind.

"I thought about driving into Rheem Valley nine years ago," Kopay said, "on my way to my first 49ers camp at St. Mary's. Then, I thought, I feel the same, only I know more now."

Kopay came from the New Orleans Saints to the Raiders last week with offensive lineman Remi Prudhomme for two future draft choices. They were among first-day arrivals at camp yesterday.

"I'm very happy about the trade," said Kopay, who is used to them after playing with four other pro teams. "Trades are a part of football, just something you have to accept. I've had great experiences every place I've been."

The only real disappointment of his career came when George Allen cut him from the Redskins after the exhibition season. "I was told I had made the team, but then on Wednesday before the first game started, I was released. Everyone was shocked. But that's Coach Allen for you."

It was a tremendous letdown and Kopay didn't know whether he wanted to continue chasing the game. Coach J. D. Roberts of the Saints talked him into heading south to New Orleans. But Kopay's playing time in Cajun Country was limited because of a painful shoulder separation that kept him out of practice for nearly five weeks. When he came back, he was a linebacker.

Kopay admitted he never expected to be around pro foot-

182

ball nine years after that first trip to St. Mary's. "I didn't see how anybody could play nine years," he exclaimed. "But age doesn't mean anything. Look at George Blanda. John Brodie will play until well past 40. And Charlie Kreuger might never retire. I hope I'm that fortunate."

[After the training camp at Oakland, Kopay was "put on waivers"—cut—but he was picked up by the Green Bay Packers in time for the regular 1972 season.]

Wisconsin State Journal, Oct. 18, 1972: TRAVELED KOPAY HOPES HE'S HOME. Dave Kopay, a widely traveled athlete, has been a 49er, a Lion, a Redskin, and a Saint during a nine-year National Football League tour. Now a Packer, the well-spoken Chicago native feels he may be home at last.

"I've been on all the special units since I came into the League nine years ago," he cheerfully reports, "and if you just count covering kickoffs, I think I've set a record. But that's part of football and it's an important part. Besides, when you're getting paid for something, you'd better do the job. And if you enjoy it, that's all the better. I wouldn't have been around as long as I have if I didn't enjoy it."

This positive attitude, plus sound intelligence and a wealth of experience, have quickly endeared Kopay to the Packer coaching staff. "Dave's a veteran and knows what he's doing in all situations," offensive backfield coach Red Cochran notes. "And he's a coachable kid—he looks younger than he actually is so you think of him as being younger. He's an accomplished football player."

Press-Gazette, Green Bay, Wis.: PACKER KAMIKAZE EYES SKINS. "It is known that the Redskins have the best special teams around the league," says the Pack's Dave Kopay, who was a Redskin in 1969, '70 and a portion of '71. Kopay, now in his ninth year as a suicide squad member and thus something of an authority on the subject, says emphasis is the key to the Redskins' skill in this area.

Despite the Redskins' reputation for excellence in these

specialties, Kopay indicated he and his fellow kamikazes will not be going into Sunday's collision with a collective inferiority complex. "I think our special teams are playing as well as anybody's right now," he said. "We're well organized and we have determined guys. And pride—the feeling that you have an obligation to the team.

"Plus," he added with great practicality, "you get paid for it."

Press-Gazette, Green Bay, Wis.—July 26, 1973, Lee Remmel column: Dave Kopay, the itinerant halfback, is what his Packer colleagues might call a "different kind of cat." A meditative type, he can most often be found exploring a book on philosophy during his free time, especially a tome on the most current thought.

That is not the only quality which sets this free-thinking Californian apart. For Kopay, one of a rare and vanishing breed, 1973 is "a magic year." If he weathers the intense competition now manifest in the Packer backfield, he will become a 10-year man in the National Football League.

David, who will discuss any subject at the drop of a helmet, is happy to explain the significance this figure has for him. "For me, it's kind of a goal very few ball players reach," he says, "especially very few backs. Plus the fact that they said it couldn't be done by a free agent. How many 10-year running backs can you name just offhand," Kopay asks rhetorically.

"It helps to play another year, too, because of the pension fund. But the big thing is playing 10 years. So few running backs stay around that long. The speed aspect is part of it—the fact of slowing as the years go by. And the pounding you get. Even if you're not starting, you still get a certain amount of pounding.

"I think I still have the same enthusiasm for the game as I did as a rookie—maybe not for the practices as much, but for the games. I know that the workouts I did in the off-season I could never have done as a rookie. I wouldn't have tried to do them. I never could run more than a mile as a rookie. This year, I ran five, six and seven miles during the off-season in California," says Dave, a muscular and bronzed blue-eyed blond who looks like the leading man in a beach party movie.

"I want to play ball here," he said quietly. "I want to finish here. I have thought that when I make the team, this would be my last year. That," he amended with a faint smile, "is if and when I make the team."

Seattle Times—Georg Meyers column: Dave Kopay seems blithely ignorant of his shortcomings, which may explain why he is now looking forward to his 10th season in the NFL. ·

"Yeah, I want to play a couple more years," he acknowledged yesterday. "It was a great experience playing at Green Bay last year. I love the game. I've had injuries and I've really been kicked around a lot. But if you really love what you're doing, you become pretty determined to make good."

And the word "determined" probably describes Dave Kopay better than any other. He has been traded three times, always for a "future draft choice." On two occasions, he was given his outright release, but still found a job.

"They say your future is programmed at an early age," Dave said. "All I ever wanted to do was play football. That's really why I was at the University of Washington. Of course, I wanted to get an education, too, but I think my real education in life has come through my experience in football."

Twenty-Four

ONE afternoon in Green Bay I got word during practice that there was an urgent message for me in the Packers business office. It was a call from Ted Robinson's father. "Dave," he said, "I know how much you cared for Ted. We don't know how it happened but he's been killed in Vietnam. They told us he was with the CIA."

After the game that week, I flew in for Ted's funeral. I was clearly the grieving lover, or at least I felt it. Whatever Ted and I might have felt for each other would never be explained now. My feelings of loss were all the more intense because of the unexplained way he had been killed in a war that didn't make sense to me. Why had he kept going back to that place? Later some friends would call this a "suicidal urge" on Ted's part. I think I'll always feel that it had something to do with Ted's repression of his true sexual feelings. He couldn't deal with my affection for him. He couldn't deal with the same feelings that must have been inside him. And so he kept going back to the war until these feelings were dead, until he was dead along with them. A man at the funeral home said Ted had been shot in the head. The CIA, of course, never had to explain who did it or how it happened, much less why.

I finished out that season with Green Bay and reported back for training camp the next year. This would be my tenth year in the NFL. I was already qualified for a pension after five years, but it would have been a good deal more after ten years.

I came back determined to play and I had a very good training camp. The cuts had all been made and my name was still on the roster. The next day, after the usual deadline for cuts, Coach Dan Devine sent one of his assistants with the message for me to turn in my playbook. I was too disgusted to try to find out why.

I went to my locker and got my stuff. Several of the other players were in a huddle talking about it. They were surprised; they were also feeling how easily it could have been one of them. Gale Gillingham, the all-pro captain of the team, put his arm around me and said, "Dave, he doesn't have any idea what he's doing. You definitely deserve to be here."

Carroll Dale, one of the all-time great players at Green Bay, a flanker back in his fourteenth year, was also cut that day. I went to my hotel and called Carroll, who had been sort of unofficial captain of the team. "Here I am in my tenth season, you'd think I'd be prepared for this." "What about me?" he said. "How do you think this makes me feel?" Carroll said Devine had convinced him to come back that year. "He told me I wouldn't be embarrassed by being cut at the last minute, that he wanted my playing and leadership on the team." Devine had used almost exactly the same words when he asked me to come back.

That year Dale went on to start for the Minnesota Vikings, who won twelve games and got to the Super Bowl. The Packers won four and lost ten.

Both of us had wanted to finish our careers playing for Green Bay. My salary was up to $32,000 by then and the money was important too. Instead I finished up the season by going back to the Oakland Raiders, this time as a member of the taxi squad—players kept in reserve in case a regular team member gets knocked out by injuries. The Raiders had agreed to pay all my expenses and $1,500 a week for three weeks. The third check never came, and I still have a grievance filed against the team through the NFL Players Association.

The next year the World Football League was forming and I took a cash bonus of $4,000 to sign on with the California

Suns, but the whole thing was so disorganized I got tired of being told what to do by coaches who didn't know as much about the game as I did, so I quit the team. They said they would try to trade me but none of the other teams was interested.

My life as a professional football player was over. When I was able to think at all about the next step, the most logical one was to take the only job I was truly qualified for—coaching. Howard Mudd was then—and still is—offensive line coach with the San Diego Chargers. He visited me and talked about my possibilities as a coach. Mudd and I had been roommates during a part of the time we were playing for the San Francisco Forty-Niners, and I was best man at his wedding. By the time of his visit in 1973 I could level with him about my homosexuality. He wasn't at all bothered by it and said he would try to help me get a job as a coach. "But for God's sake," he said, "don't tell anybody you're gay or you'll never get a job."

But there were too many people who knew by then. And besides, I was tired of hiding, sick of playing games about who I really wanted to be with. Anyhow, no coaching job ever materialized. Nobody was ever specific in explaining why my applications and inquiries weren't acknowledged. But I know it has to be the widespread knowledge of my homosexuality. My record speaks for itself, and I think it's fair to say it qualifies me for any number of coaching positions that have come vacant in the past three years.

Neither of the two business ventures I invested in worked out either, but my social life was better than it had ever been. I worked out nearly every day at UCLA. One friend was a strikingly handsome man who had been a member of the American Olympic team one year. He and I had been friends for a long time but I had never been able to tell him the sexual attraction I felt for him. When I finally did he said he was flattered and wanted to do something about it but he couldn't deal with it as a direct homosexual experience. His suggestion was that we find a woman to share it with us.

It happened that I did have a special woman friend who was very free sexually. She made it with women, but preferred sex with men, especially athletes. She had always told me more than once that she wanted to make it with me and another man. So the three of us got together. I was, this time, naturally aroused by her and I think the reason was my knowing that she was also turned on by other women. Somehow knowing this made being with her easier, made it easier to respond to her. She had told me that only a woman could really know another woman and that was why she could understand the intensity of my feelings for other men. She also said she had once been afraid of making love with a woman because it would be so intense she would never want to have sex with a man afterward, but then she discovered that this wasn't true, that the more freely she expressed herself with women the more relaxed she seemed to feel around men.

With her there, my friend was able to be as excited by me as he was by her. The pleasures of regular intercourse, oral sex and simply caressing each other were shared by all three of us. In a way it was one of the most complete sexual experiences I had ever known.

There were other sex partners that I met at that time. One—still a close friend—was a singer and basketball player. He is six feet eight, slender, has dark hair and a smooth, hairless body. Later he was one of the most popular subjects in the Colt Studios series of nude photographs.

After her divorce my sister Marguerite decided to move up to Sun Valley, Idaho, and I helped her move and decided to stay there for three or four months myself. Finally I decided I had to go back to Washington. I told myself the decision had to do with the small business I was trying to organize selling NFL pub-style bar mirrors. But I know there was more to it than that. Washington had been the scene of so many changes in my life, I'm sure I was going there expecting still another one.

I arrived back in Washington in late November 1975. In a matter of days I would read the first article in *The Washington Star* series on homosexuals in sports. And I would know as I was reading it that my life would never be the same.

Twenty-Five

THE letters I received in the year after my "coming out" in the *Star* series have brought tremendous comfort and encouragement. They tell me about other people out there still suffering in the confusion I once knew. They tell me that it is important for someone like me to speak out. Most important, they carry the message I was so desperate to hear myself: that we are not alone.

The following excerpts are printed with the permission of the people who wrote these letters. Many of the letters themselves explain why some of them requested that their names not be published.

Dear Dave,

You took a difficult and controversial subject and treated it with quiet dignity and a firmness to be applauded. I know many men who are caught up with the macho bit to the extent they cringe if a man puts a hand on their shoulder in a gesture of goodwill and if one were to say they could possibly love someone of the same gender, they would turn away in disgust. These same men will tell you of their sexual prowess but they don't know how to make love. When I was in college the captain of the football team was considered all man. He did everything athletes were supposed to do except for one night when he helped me into bed after a night out with the men, and then proceeded to make love to me. After the initial shock, I allowed myself to enjoy what he was doing and I enjoyed his lovemaking again and again for over a five-month period until he graduated and left the area. I consider myself a man and I consider what happened between the two of us a beautiful thing.

Dear Dave Kopay,

I am a 36 year old lesbian, a poet who has just published my first book, and a teacher of English at Brooklyn College. I came out later in life than I might have, for although I was aware of homosexual feelings for many years, I denied that part of myself because the heterosexual hard sell of the society (my family in particular) and the stigma attached to homosexuality convinced me that I was someone other than myself. After two years of therapy with a very sensitive and beautiful therapist, and with the help and support of courageous friends, I decided to come out publicly as well as to tell my family that I'm a lesbian. There's been some pain and some rejection—my mother simply can't deal with it—and yet it was the most freeing act of my life to be able to say this is who I am. One of the things you said that I most appreciated was that our society is about the differences among us. It is the very essence of civilization, I think, and to deny difference or not permit it will make us less able to survive our future as humans.

I have an eight-year-old daughter and I will respect whatever her sexuality is and whatever choices she makes as her own; and I think she is benefitting from her awareness of a full range of human sexual (and other) possibilities, and from the respect for difference that exists in our life. I was just interviewed by Geraldo Rivera for an ABC News story on gay parents. Mostly, Rivera seemed neutral during the interview, but when he was leaving my house he said he still hadn't made up his own mind whether or not homosexuality was "normal," or whether children suffered from having gay parents. It struck me later that if I had been black, he would never have had the nerve to say to my face "I still haven't made up my mind whether or not black people are really shiftless and lazy." It's very hard to keep on sticking your neck out in the face of that kind of backwardness, but I think it helps to do it: I was strengthened by the memory of your dignity and self-respect on the Susskind show.

Sincerely, Joan Larkin, Brooklyn, N.Y.

Dear Dave Kopay,

I wish I could justify coming out to myself for I am a graduate physical education student (exercise physiology), an oarsman for the crew club and I coach the local prep school crews. I want either to go to med school ultimately heading for sports medicine or get a doctorate to teach and coach on a college level. I tend to think the latter will be my course and I do not want to declare my homosexuality until I have reached a position important enough to carry weight. If I reach the national championships next year in rowing, maybe I'll have enough guts to declare my gayness. All I can say in conclusion is that thank God someone with your credentials had the guts to "come out" so that others know we can function as successful athletes.

Dear Dave Kopay,

I just finished watching (Wow) your appearance on the Tomorrow Show with Tom Snyder. Allow me to say that your coming out has been a real source of encouragement and joy to me. I hope you can keep up your courage, and especially your love, and your altruistic sense of values. I almost wish you needed whatever I have to give. My heart is beating a little faster right now. It's just neat being able to say these things. I'm 37, a priest for 12 years. In [. . .], a country parish where I've really got to watch myself. Carefully. There's a man in the parish, exactly my age, who really likes me, and I like him. But he will marry because it's "the thing to do." That is common around here, where those who don't marry are suspect. I'm trying to be what I am as a person, and hopefully will be able to remain a priest. But both may not be possible. Say a prayer for me, please. Or just remember the name in a prayer you say for someone else. God and many others love you.

Dear Dave:

When I was in high school in the early 60s, I was just beginning to realize what my sexuality really was. I realized that I was growing more and more interested in and attracted to my own sex. Of course, I became frightened and bewildered and tried to see if there were others like me, although quite positive that I was the only one. I secretly read everything I could find in magazines on homosexuality. I discreetly gleaned the libraries for information. From this and my peers it all boiled down to the "fact" that homosexuals were effeminate sick people. But I didn't see myself this way. I didn't see myself like the "queers" jeered at at school. Yet if I was that way then I must be like them. The confusion grew and compounded. The more I learned and read the more mixed up I became. Boy, how my heart would swell with pride when the coach, chemistry teacher or boss would tell me I was "typical all boy." But with the pride came the panic that I was the lone exception. The tragic thing is that I am just recently realizing the falsity of this. For years I have been alone because I too believed the myths. I bought the whole pile of garbage without question. Gay people are just as much the believers and victims of society's myths about them as straights. All people—gay as well as straight—must realize that the only common denominator among gays is and only is an emotional and physical attraction for their own sex.

Dear David Kopay,

Bravo to you for your courage. Courage is more than a quarterback averting a tackle; it is also moving into the public arena and stating who you are. Thousands you will never meet will be a little more self-accepting because someone, with whom they can identify, has spoken out. As a kid, always a lover and participant of sports, I felt alone. I never had the role model for honest delving into my feelings as you have now offered.

Two years ago, when I went public on the David Susskind Show, my job as director of an ex-convict self-help program was "news" because the area is obtrusively macho. I thought that I was putting everything on the line, because, for years, I had heard locker room "fag putdowns." What I hadn't heard were the silences of many straight people who did not feel threatened or angered by a different sexual orientation. My fears were formulated from the noisy, nervous few. So, when the word came out about my being "gay," I was not prepared for the acceptance from so many people, longtime friends and work associates as well as public figures. We, too long, have believed that we would be rejected and never knew that ac-

ceptance was possible. I hope that you will find peace and happiness
and can listen to the silences of people who will accept you.

Cordially,
David Rothenberg
Executive director
The Fortune Society
New York City

Dear Dave,

I hope you will remember me from the minor seminary. I have
not seen you for about twelve years since on one occasion when you
came to Claretville to visit some of your classmates. I was in the
class ahead of you. It will be two years this June since I came out
myself, though I had been rationalizing about my own sexual orientation for almost twenty years. Presently I am teaching sophomore
religion in a boys military academy. Needless to say, therefore, I
cannot be as much of an activist in these circumstances as I would
like to be. However, neither do I have to put on any pretense of
being straight, since the issue hardly ever arises. Were it to, I am
certain I would take my stand and, of course, lose my job, but I have
always realized this possibility since I took the job and like to think
that I would have the last laugh, since on all accounts I do a very rep-
utable job of teaching. Last year, I had hoped to get more into the
thick of battle. However, there are a number of other areas in my life
which call for support, and following my present line of action seems
to be the only viable way right now. I know that we are faced with a
massive need for education of the public. Perhaps its massiveness
alone justifies a variety of more or less public positions.

Dear Dave

I just had to tell you that listening to you talk for an hour on the
Susskind Show has done more toward helping me accept myself
than all the reading and thinking I've ever done, and almost as much
as all the sessions I've had with my wise and understanding
therapist. Your appearance on the show coincided with a very important point in my own process of coming out. Of all the "depro-

gramming" I have to do, the hardest part of it has been ridding my-self of the notion that homosexuality is just one messed-up facet of an even more messed-up personality. But after one hour of being exposed to your warmth, your compassion, your sensitivity, and, above all, your courage, I found myself thinking, "My God, this guy makes being gay seem positively noble." I had to think about this for quite a while; that must have been the last adjective I ever thought I'd apply to homosexuality. Finally, I realized that nothing could possibly be more noble than to be a complete human being, at peace with himself, free to love and able to love.

David—Glad to hear things are going your way—now that you're "notorious" or whatever. Why didn't you ever tell me? Ha!

All this time I just thought you were a chickenshit football player . . . Take Care.

[Much to his surprise, this friend—who works for National Foot-ball League Properties, Inc.—was told by his boss not to publish his name in connection with this letter to me. In a very small way, he experienced something homosexuals go through every day.]

Dear Mr. Kopay:

I'm one of Iowa's current crop of young farmers: single, somewhat educated and possessing an affection for tennis. To know me is to know my farm. It's large by Iowa standards but not front page copy. At the very least I'm competent at my work. If you have never been on an Iowa farm, be advised that it's a great place to be—splendid solitude. In as much as farmers are self-employed, personal prefer-ence is of little importance. So long as my corn rows are planted straight, I'm accepted by my neighbors.

Dear Mr. Kopay:

Having long admired your skill during your years as a 49er, I am even more your fan since reading the recent *Washington Star* arti-cle in the green pages of *The San Francisco Chronicle*. Gay myself for some time, I have only recently become comfortable enough with that gayness so that I've quit worrying about what others may think about me, secure as I am in the awareness of my manhood.

The difficulty of your current position I can pretty well guess. As a high school English teacher, I would like openly to serve as a model for those of my students I either know or suspect are also gay but may be having difficulty dealing with it. As yet, I haven't seen my way clear to make an open declaration to them; perhaps after all, high school may not be the place for such outspokenness. I really don't know. All the more reason, I guess, why your decision excites my admiration as much—no, more—than did your exploits on the football field. With gratitude, love and best wishes.

Dear Dave:

I saw you on the David Susskind Show. I wish you luck in getting the coaching job. If you ever need signatures for a poll on how many parents would have you coach their sons, I would sign for my three sons. I feel a person's personal life has nothing to do with the merits of his ability to work. I hope I can be as strong as you.

> Best wishes,
> Frances Mecca
> Howard Beach, N.Y.

Dave (O.K.?)

You did more for me in that one 45-minute television interview than I've been able to do in almost a year of soul-searching and selective conversation. I'm a 19 year old guy with a semi-steady girl, an exclusively heterosexual past and—until recently—a presumably heterosexual future. Recently a guy I've known at school for about a year and a half has begun making rather blunt overtures—sexually—in my direction. Shit. All these big words. He's been putting "the move" on me. And I've been very casually sidestepping them. Which is fine except I'm not at all sure I want to sidestep them. So it's been really bugging me. I've talked it over with him, tried to explain it to him, but I don't know how or what to say to my girl, my one real love right now. Last night, we had our closest yet to a discussion of it—and although it never came out, I think she now realizes what the problem is. I got home and turned on the TV feeling really down and man—THERE YOU WERE! I just sat there and didn't move for an hour. I hung on your every word. You seem so at peace with yourself and able to articulate things I've been trying to tell myself and others for months now. Man you almost made me cry and that isn't too usual for me. I called the guy today and I'm gonna see him for a long talk next weekend. I need that much time to prepare myself because I guess it'll be a turning point in my life. So something's gonna happen and for the first time in quite a while—although I'm nervous as hell—I feel good about myself, my sexuality. It's me and I have no reason or right to deny it. I love you and I thank you. No shit.

David,

As you know, I'm sure, you're big news all over! I thought I'd write a quick note and lend some support if you need it and tell you that I was moved by your courage and candor. I hope that all the feedback you've gotten has been supportive and positive—but then I have always been a romantic optimist. It sounds as though you'd like to find work in football somehow but the doors were getting closed instead of opened—the puritan mentality always has prevailed in that business. How about other things?

As I read back over this thing it sounds silly and trite and doesn't say all that I'd like, but I am hoping that things are going as you'd like and I did want to let you know that I was thinking of you. I'm in school full time now—stop by and see us if you get in this direction.

Malcolm Snider, Stoughton, Michigan

[Malcolm Snider, who is now in medical school, played offensive guard for the Atlanta Falcons and for the Green Bay Packers. His was the only letter I received from any of my former pro football teammates.]

Dear Dave:

Your coming out publicly will help a lot of people, especially kids who find themselves confused, scared and alone. It's time someone spoke up and dispelled the myths that exist in the sports world about homosexuality. I've been watching the first week of new television shows and am pleasantly surprised at the number of gay characters showing up—and, for the most part, being presented in a

198

positive light. Last night on "Alice" there was a "gay ex-pro quarter-back" and that has to be a direct result of your having come out. It must give you a good feeling to see such tangible changes taking place and to know you've helped bring them about.

My background is somewhat similar to yours. I was a competitive swimmer for nine years—in high school, prep school and college—and grew up in a Catholic sports family. My father has been my hometown high school basketball and baseball coach for 20-some years, my mother teaches gym and swimming. I was well aware of the homosexual taboo in sports. I didn't really begin to admit to myself I was gay till my last year in college. After that, I was secretive about my sex lives, but three years ago I came out to my family and friends. It was hard to do, but went pretty well. My family's accepted it, tho my parents are still nervous about other people in town knowing or finding out. I now live in New York, trying to build careers as an actor and a writer. My open gayness may result in some obstacles, particularly with the idea of an actor's "public image," but the pressure of staying in the closet would have been unbearable. Hang in there and good luck. I'm enclosing one of my poems:

Golden-haired, tanned, Amherst bodies
trained for weeks in Lauderdale sun,
leanly muscled,
smoothly slicing through choppy waters . . .

for years
I swam against bodies,
men's bodies of all types,

admiring them for the times they did,
for being good competitors,
for being personalities

but never for their bodies:

I had been well trained.
> —Michael O'Connor

V

Twenty-Six

COLLABORATORS in life now, Kopay and Young set off across America. A journey of 9,000 miles was to take them back to the major characters and settings in this book. The climax of the trip was to be the annual May Alumni game in Seattle. That would be the first time Kopay had confronted his former teammates, coaches and fans since his public discussions of homosexuality. Along the way, Kopay would also be facing the members of his family—his grandmother and aunts in Chicago, his older brother who said he had cost him the head coaching job at Oregon State, his father who said he would kill him, his mother who said she never wanted to see him again.

Two tempestuous egos—the writer's and the professional athlete's—and their six-foot-plus frames were jammed uncomfortably into a tiny Toyota pickup for thirty days. Sleeping in the same motel rooms and trapped as traveling companions, they came to know each other as few people ever do. Overwhelming their personal exchanges was the constant dialogue over the words and phrases that would be used in this book.

They were opposites only on the surface. Here was Kopay, born on the South Side of Chicago, reared in Los Angeles, his whole life the story of the American athlete. And here was Young, born and reared on a truck farm in the mountains of North Carolina, a sissy in his childhood who played the piano instead of sports. Just in the day-to-day predicaments of travel, they came to appreciate each other's differences, but, more important, to discover the very real similarities in their lives. It was important to Kopay that Young not just hear his story and record it, but that he understand it as well. This took a lot of explaining—and, sometimes, arguing.

With ten days to drive from Washington, D.C., to Seattle, Washington, Kopay was as anxious at the start of the trip as if he had only minutes to make it to the team bus. He ordered Young to be waiting on the sidewalk in five minutes, they had to get on the road. "Listen," Young said, "we've got almost two weeks to get there. You don't have to be so fucking anxious you keep us from enjoying the trip."

Stubborn, even eccentric—when it came to the daily routine of his life—Young wasn't easily given to compromise. He decided, though, that the project itself was worth it and the trip would provide some very useful lessons about living with another person at least as complicated as himself.

Kopay arrived, contrite, half an hour later. The two locked arms, and began the trip laughing, a little uneasily. Maybe they were caught in a circle in which the anxiety of one presupposed—and caused—the anxiety in the other. Both of them were reassuring themselves that at least it would be a tremendous learning experience.

The day was clear and sunny, blue skies right down to the rolling pasturelands of Maryland, a fresh rich green, the third week in April. The two of them and a college boy in a little sports car convertible waved back and forth all the way to the first exit to Pittsburgh.

Even with days to spare, Kopay allowed no time for restroom stops, and there were only two meals each day—breakfast before starting and dinner after they had stopped at night. Getting there was the all-important consideration to him—never mind that he had no reason to be in a hurry, no set time to arrive. Kopay and his wife had staged a similar trip in the same pickup just six months earlier and it had caused the final break in their relationship. "I'm tired of being treated like a piece of your baggage," she had told him. It was a line Young himself was to use midway through the trip. She had also asked Young—during that luncheon interview in New

York—"Did you really think he was going to kill you when he looked that way?" She had thought he would and so had Young.

What would cause that look of absolute rage? A wrong turn or a question worded in a way that offended Kopay. At first he was so easily offended Young didn't dare indulge in his usual brand of sarcastic humor. It was healthy, Young figured, for him to have to cut back on his sarcasm because much of it was rooted in condescension. If Young were condescending about Kopay's preoccupation with a life of ball scores, he had to know that his own career of reporting on the "more serious" games—demonstrations, wars, riots, politics—had amounted to considerably more dehumanized statistics than those on the sports pages. In fact, he decided, journalism would be a much higher calling if the other reporters approached their subjects with the same critical scrutiny the better sports writers used in describing their players and games.

Once, when Kopay was stopped for speeding, that look came over his face. Young was terrified that Kopay would actually threaten the officer who had stopped him. There were quick visions of Kopay lunging for the man and getting shot or jailed for assault. And there Young would be without a valid driver's license in a Toyota pickup a hundred miles from the nearest town.

The fine was ridiculously small compared to the offense, but Kopay's rage had left him speechless—and that was the only thing that saved him. He said he had wanted to destroy that officer, but he had been in the wrong and he knew it. Maybe that was at least a partial explanation for his rage. Always trying to be first—or right—could be a compelling, and perhaps destructive, force in every serious athlete. And Kopay had been a serious athlete.

Uncomfortable as the lessons were, Young was learning something of the workings of the athlete's mind. Slowly, as a friend but also as one interested in a very different mind at work, Young would ask Kopay about his anxiety and about this irrational rage of his. Sometime after the speeding arrest Young said to Kopay: "If I had wanted to kill that man the way you did I would try to figure it out, try to do something about the way I felt."

It was maybe the first time Kopay had ever been questioned about these feelings in such detail. Sometimes these discussions were as exhausting as real fistfights. Young always had in mind that it wasn't enough for them to think and talk about all this, at a certain point they would also have to write it down in a way that made sense on the printed page. While Kopay didn't always respond immediately to these questions—and outright accusations—he never forgot them. Months after Young had mentioned something, Kopay would come back with the answers he had carefully considered in that time.

Some of the strongest memories I have from my childhood involve the intense competition I got into with my buddies in St. Patrick's grade school. Whether it was basketball, kickball, football or even Ping-Pong, we were so obsessed with winning we would often end up in fistfights and the sisters would have to rush in and stop us.

This obligation to win, to be first, was part of my life from the time of my first involvement with sports. The joy of the game has too often been affected by this attitude that took hold of me at a very early age. As college and professional football have become big business, Lombardi's "winning isn't everything, it's the only thing" has taken over as a dehumanized commercial slogan to be lived up to or else.

I remember a game with the Chicago Bears during my rookie year with the Forty-Niners. I had played very well—rushed ninety-nine yards in nineteen carries, caught six passes—but afterward I felt guilty that I was feeling good. The team had lost, and that was what mattered. That was all that mattered.

On one level we all appreciated or at least gave lip service to Grantland Rice's famous lines . . . "When the One Great Scorer comes to mark against your name—He writes—not that you won or lost—but how you played the Game." But on the gut level of actually playing the game, we knew this wasn't true no matter how nice the words sounded.

Now I think it could be true, now I believe that the true athlete doesn't have to be obsessed with being number one. The coaches, I think, have done a great deal of damage to athletes in this area. They think they can succeed—meaning win—only by intimidation, by demanding the impossible "hundred and ten per cent."

I know it doesn't have to be this way. I've played for coaches, successful winning coaches—Chesty Walker at the University of Washington, Jack Christiansen at the San Francisco Forty-Niners, Don Dole and Bart Starr at Green Bay, and Chuck Knox at Detroit—who helped players develop their skills right up to the limit of their potential without making them feel like failures—less than a man—for not reaching impossible goals.

It would be nice to be able to say I've overcome all this competitiveness. I haven't. It's not so easy to change after a lifetime of identifying with rigid attitudes like these. There have even been times since I started talking publicly about my homosexuality when I have been an even fiercer competitor than I was before. I know what's going on here and I'm trying to change—because it's still destroying too much of my enjoyment of the game. Playing a pickup game of basketball with some friends in the afternoon—it becomes even more important for me to win, to be the most dominant player on the court. Knowing they all know I am homosexual adds pressure—in my mind at least—for me to show them I am "more a man" than they are.

Since I started working on this book I've tried to deal with questions like this as I never in my life did before. I recognize the absurdity of being so fierce among friendly people in what should be a game. I've learned that when I'm not so crazy about winning, about being first, I not only enjoy the game more, I become a far better player.

It was a grueling trip straight through from Washington to Chicago with stops only for gas. Kopay and Young separated almost as soon as they arrived. Kopay went off with a young man he enjoyed having sex with and Young spent a pleasant evening with a former lover in his apartment near the top of the Hancock Tower.

With words such as "compulsive" and "anxiety" out in the open, Kopay seemed more relaxed the next morning. Just defining those words seemed a first step toward easing the tension between them. Young had planned an Easter feast in a favorite Greek restaurant in Chicago, but he knew that Kopay was uncomfortable, wanting to get back on the road. Before they left Chicago they stopped at a filling station where Kopay called his grandmother—whose home was only five minutes from where they were.

I had not talked to my grandmother since the stories about my homosexuality had come out. However, all of my aunts had written me and said they didn't want Grandmother to find out, that they had kept the newspapers away from her whenever there was any mention of me in them.

I was honestly confused by this. I loved my grandmother, I knew she loved me and I had reason to believe she would be more understanding than my aunts thought she would be. While my grandmother had been very strict with her own children—so strict three of my aunts never married; one became a nun and two still live at home—she had mellowed through the years. When my parents were being so strict with my sister—not wanting her to move out on her own—it was my grandmother who defended my sister and said our parents should be more lenient.

My aunts asked me how I had been and I told them it had been a pretty rough time—especially without my family's support. Except for the one letter from each of them, there had been no communication at all between us, and that was unusual because I had always been very close to my aunts and my grandmother.

There was no mention of homosexuality. I couldn't even talk about being on the television shows or doing a book. They didn't want grandmother to know any of that, and I felt I had to go along.

When Grandmother came on the phone she teased me as she always had. "David, are you being a good boy? You aren't doing anything I wouldn't do?" I told her that the only reason she wasn't doing anything was because she was too old. She laughed. And that was the end of conversation. None of them asked me to come by.

That was the first time I had ever been in Chicago without going by my grandmother's house. Before, I wouldn't even have called. I would have just rung the doorbell and walked on in. After all, it had been a home to me all my life. My visits had been a special occasion to them. My grandmother is a fabulous cook and she loved to see me eating huge helpings of whatever she had fixed. There was always a roast and fresh bread and cake or pie brought out in honor of my visit.

To look over the area where I grew up we turned off the expressway and found the old neighborhood I had been trying to describe to Young. The white frame house my parents had owned looked very tiny compared to what I remembered. The new owners had cut down the lilac bushes.

We drove past St. Christina's church and school, past what had been a farmhouse when I lived there. Then we pulled into the White Castle and had four delicious hamburgers all the way. Afterward I pointed out the brick house where my grandmother lived, where all of my Chicago relatives would be gathered around a big Easter dinner.

We passed on by, headed south on the expressway, then due west across the open flatlands of Iowa. The farmers were turning the soil for the first time that spring. A radio reporter said they were late sowing this year because of the weather.

It seemed like there was nothing left for me in Chicago, and I told myself I was glad to be leaving the place behind me. There's a kind of freedom that comes with moving on.

Twenty-Seven

YOUNG was the navigator and secretary—holding the maps, keeping track of expenses, mileage, tapes and notebooks. Kopay was in charge. This was fine with Young, who had owned only one car in his life and —after losing it several nights in a row—sold it because he hated the hassles it brought into his life.

An incurable rambler, Young had been all over Europe, Scandinavia, the near, middle and far East. Except for his brief trip to Acapulco, Kopay had never left the U.S.A. Still, he had been as restless as Young—driving back and forth across the country two and sometimes three and four times a year.

When the two checked into a motel, Kopay always signed his name for the room. Likewise, he got the choice of beds, decided what time they would get up.

Since a great deal of their talk was about Kopay's sex life, Young had to be especially careful about comparing it to his own. Casual sex had become a way of life for Young and he wasn't particular where he found a brief sex partner. Kopay had once said, "I worry about your promiscuity," and Young had laughed, because the truth was that Kopay had had no more of a marriage-type sexual relationship than Young. But he held to the romantic belief that somewhere there was a perfect person just for him. By this time in his life, Young had decided that for him this attitude killed more good relationships than it encouraged. He had given up on the notion of finding a perfect mate, although he still hoped to find a best friend who wanted to share a house and a life without demanding sexual fidelity. Promiscuity today, Young felt, was a realistic component of many kinds of sexual relations. It was, after all, a wandering eye that brought many modern couples together. Why should the same casual meeting with another pair of eyes destroy a meaningful relationship. To apply the idealized heterosexual definitions of a "relationship" to a homosexual partnership seemed unrealistic and likely to limit its endurance.

After some time together Kopay and Young were able to talk more, and with more ease, about sex. And along the way Kopay gradually began to talk with uncharacteristic openness about what he really wanted and expected from his sexuality.

What has happened is that I am now more honest in my response to the people I meet and want to be with. If I am sexually attracted to a man or a woman I no longer have to worry about telling them.

I am no more or less lonely than other single people I know. I still hope to find a "main man," a meaningful sexual relationship with a best friend. I also don't rule out the possibility of getting involved with a woman again and having children. But at this time in my life what I want most is a real commitment of love with another man. Of course there was never even the possibility of finding such a man when I wasn't honest about who I was and wanted to become. I had to know myself better, and be more at ease with myself, before I could think about sharing with another person. I feel this is a process everybody should go through, but with the help of various masks a lot of us never do.

As an athlete I knew I had a certain potential for performing better than others. In order to develop this I knew I had to struggle and to fight—often overcoming real fear and pain. Emotionally, I've had a similar struggle in finding my true sexual identity. I always had the potential for the natural and honest expression of myself sexually, but I was never able to do it. I was held back by inhibitions put on me and accepted by me from the church, my family, the sports establishment and the larger one beyond it.

It turned out that Kopay was not entirely as rigid in his behavior as he was, at first, in his talk. He seemed to have a name and number for nearly every town the two visited. After Kopay came back from a visit with one such friend, Young looked at him and laughed: "Kopay, I'm really worried about your promiscuity . . ."

As they headed west across Wyoming, they were overcome by huge clouds that seemed to be clutching at them with gigantic hands. Straight ahead, though, was a shaft of sunlight that seemed to be providing a path for them just ahead of a violent storm they could see in the rear-view mirrors. Meanwhile Kopay played the soundtrack from *Jonathan Livingston Seagull* and described how the movie star gull had sailed so freely in and out of the clouds. That, he said, was why so many athletes had been taken by the story. Every time Kopay played that tape, Young was allowed to hear the rock opera *Tommy*—all of it.

They stayed overnight in the little town of Sidney, Wyoming, where they woke up to a huge country breakfast with freshly baked sweet rolls as big as two fists. They slowed down at the edge of town to watch a beautiful pair of pheasants pecking in a field. During the whole trip they were forever commenting on every new plant and animal they saw. As for plants and flowers, Kopay kept saying, "Just wait until you see Seattle—the begonias! You won't believe how beautiful they are." Young, who had helped raise thousands of begonias in his parents' greenhouses back in North Carolina, stayed quiet. But he couldn't understand how that tiny flower could seem so spectacular to Kopay.

In Salt Lake City Kopay called a young man he knew and they went off to play handball. Young took in a minute or so of the guided tour through Mormon Square, including the part about seagulls showing up to save the Mormons from a plague of crickets. "Crickets?" asked an old fellow in Bermuda shorts, winking at Young. At the gay bar three blocks away, the bartender said, "Yeah, we got a lot of crickets in Salt Lake City."

Early the next morning they headed due north to Idaho, passing by the deep blue waters of the Great Salt Lake, and through the flat fields that stretched straight to the base of steep, snow-covered mountains. Further north there were tumbleweeds caught in the barbed wire along the road, and Young was thinking of himself as caught like that because Kopay was raging at him over some innocent question about the possible sexual significance of the football uniform. Kopay said it really infuriated him— "all these gay people who don't know or care a damn about playing football coming up to me in bars and all they want to talk about is the fanny-patting and how everything shows football players are all re-pressed homosexuals." "Dammit, Kopay," Young said, "you and I are supposed to be writing a book about a search for sexual identity, not a book about how to play football." Kopay at first gave Young his famous look that could kill, then nod-ded and said turn the tape recorder back on.

At Twin Falls, Idaho, Kopay pulled off the main road to show Young the Snake River Canyon, then they headed north through huge sterile flats of lava beds toward the high, snow-covered peaks of the Sawtooth Mountains, the incredibly beautiful setting where Ernest Hemingway chose to end his life.

In what looks like a bare vacant lot just past the Ketchum Trailer Park, Hemingway is buried under a simple slab of granite inscribed only with his name, birth and death dates. Regardless of whatever he said or did in his private life, Hemingway did as much as any writer of his time to tell of the awful conflicts involved in being a man. Sexual confusion un-derscores much of the drama in his novels and stories. It seemed fitting that Kopay and Young—whose generation was so heavily influenced by Hemingway's words—should carry their own talk and discovery of manhood and sexuality into this place where he had lived and worked.

Marguerite Kopay was at her desk in a stock brokerage office just off the few blocks of Main Street in Ketchum, Idaho. She had a wholesome, athletic look herself. Her frosted blonde hair was cut short, her blue eyes sparkling, her mouth open in a wide smile of welcome for her best friend and favorite brother. They hugged and kissed; the sister welcomed Young as an old friend. A generous, mothering sort of person, Marguerite already had three people staying at her apartment but she found Kopay and Young a pleasant duplex with a view of the mountains.

That night during dinner at Marguerite's apartment Kopay and his sister's boyfriend were lost in conversation. Marguerite had worried about the boyfriend's reaction to Kopay's discussions of homosexuality, but when she finally mentioned it, the boyfriend immediately said he had a lot of questions he wanted to ask.

I told him what a country boy had told me about this whole business of sexuality. He said, "Look, we come from both a man and a woman. That means we're made of both. Shouldn't we have the feelings and needs of both a man and a woman?"

You know, I said, the major difference in the sexes is the sex organs themselves. I don't think there's really that much difference in human beings when it comes to the basic emotional needs. A man shouldn't have to flex his muscles to prove he's stronger and to assert his dominance. Why should either role be dominant? Why should the roles inhibit us from expressing what we naturally feel?

Men can be as sensitive as women, women can be as strong emotionally as men. For a man to show some feeling, even to cry, shouldn't be a sign of weakness. But in our society it's

215

often very difficult—even painful—to be who you are instead of who you're expected to be.

Marguerite was amazed that her boyfriend was so interested in Kopay's questions. It hadn't occurred to her that what troubled her brother was common to a lot of other men. While they talked, she sat reading the proposal and outline for this book, and at one point she started crying and left the table. When she came back she said, "I'm sorry, but I know these people and it's all so true for me." She was also concerned for her parents because "I have seen them age through all this. But," she added, "the book does seem to be the only way David will ever be able to explain himself to our parents. They will never accept his homosexuality, but maybe they will understand him and what he's done better through the book."

After a few days in Ketchum, Kopay and Young got back on the road, this time heading straight for Seattle. Going over the Snoqualmie Pass, they saw that the ski lifts along the road were all closed for the season, but a late spring blizzard was piling up a thick cover of snow on the mountainsides. The snow seemed to be blowing off the road as they headed up and around the high mountains, but as they neared the pass itself they could not see a car-length in front of them and the road was under a blanket of white. They had no snow tires and neither of them was about to stop to put on the chains. They kept on driving.

The blizzard finally behind them, they eased into the town of Snoqualmie Falls in the foothills. Kopay wanted to have breakfast at the lodge where he had been entertained as a potential football star by the University of Washington fifteen years earlier. Eating at the table beside them was a middle-aged man and his mother. He never looked over. But when Kopay was leaving the man followed him out and stopped him—in the lobby, where his mother couldn't see. "I saw you

216

on the Susskind show, and I had to say 'thank you' for what you're doing."

As they neared Seattle, it was Young whose anxiety began to build over the potential dangers Kopay faced. More than any physical harm, he worried about the verbal insults from strangers and the cold silence from old friends. Kopay wasn't the kind to dwell on the possibility of bad times ahead; he would deal with it when it happened. Meanwhile, he was keyed up just to be back in the place itself.

He insisted on swinging around the beltway so that Young could see the town. Over there was the racetrack, where Kopay had worked one summer. There was the Boeing plant, where the new alternate command-center plane for the President of the United States was taking off in a daily practice flight. There was the new, raw concrete King Dome where the Alumni game would be played. Up there was the Space Needle. And all around them was the water.

They came, then, to the university section of town. Kopay pulled off the expressway and eased up to a stoplight. "There's the swimming coach," Kopay said, nodding to the car in the right lane just ahead of them. "I wonder what he'd think if he saw me . . ." The sentence trailed off and Kopay stayed back until the coach had pulled out without seeing him.

Young's attention was particularly caught by the amazing variety of colors in the azaleas and rhododendrons blooming in every yard. He saw no begonias, but did not mention it.

Their host in Seattle was to be Charles Brydon, who shared a house across from the university with Dr. Harold Johnson, a psychiatrist. Brydon is the organizing force behind the Dorian Group, an active and influential association of gay professional men and women. He is also the manager of the northwest branch of AFIA-World Wide Insurance. As spokesman for the Dorian Group, Brydon is frequently identified on television and in the newspapers as a homosexual. Not only has this not hurt his career, the volume of business in his office has doubled in the time he has been a gay activist.

A genial, diplomatic sort, Brydon has also made himself and the gay community in Seattle influential with politicians. He was active in getting so-called sodomy laws rescinded in the state and, when the new law took effect in July 1976, in getting a commission appointed to consider the commutation of sentences of all persons in prison under the old laws. He was active in Seattle Mayor Wes Uhlman's unsuccessful campaign for the Democratic gubernatorial nomination. Uhlman appointed several known homosexuals to various committees and delivered an unusually strong speech for gay rights during his campaign.

Johnson, a wry, soft-spoken man, works in a clinic where a number of troubled homosexuals have sought treatment. He is also calm and open about his own homosexuality. He is skeptical about the supposed terrible consequences for those who feel to acknowledge their homosexuality would compromise them professionally. He practices what he preaches, as he indicated one night at a dinner party for Kopay during which a woman sociologist was explaining why it was necessary for her to keep secret about her bisexuality. She said it would compromise the objective nature of her studies on the subject. She also said it would have damaged her testimony as an expert witness in behalf of two lesbian lovers who were trying to get custody of one partner's children. "They asked me off the stand if I were lesbian and I told them I wouldn't answer that. I thought it would hurt their case."

Johnson spoke up: "I was an expert witness in the same case. They asked me on the witness stand if I were homosexual and I told them the truth. I don't think it hurt their case or my testimony."

Kopay had said he wanted to reserve the week before the game for practice. He wanted no interviews or publicity before the Alumni game on Saturday. After the game, on Sunday, the Dorian Group was sponsoring a dinner at the Hilton Hotel at which Kopay would speak, and more than 350 people had paid $12 each to hear him. Monday there would be a press conference and a private meeting with Mayor Uhlman. The printed schedule Brydon had prepared for the week seemed an ominous reminder of the several opportunities Kopay would have that week for being a public target.

Monday afternoon Kopay went over to the stadium for his first practice. Young, more anxious about the possible dangers than the man who had to face them, went out and got drunk. But he made sure to get back to the house in time to hear Kopay's story of what happened when he went into the locker room.

Twenty-Eight

THE first thing I had to do was check out my equipment. I went into the equipment room as I always had. There was old Harry Yalacki, who had helped me get suited up so many times before—he had taken a job with the Seattle Seahawks but was back just for the Alumni game. The first pair of pants he gave me fitted perfectly and he produced a special helmet he knew would be just right for me.

"Charlie Tuna" Talbott, another equipment man, joked about how fussy I always was about my gear. "Well," he said, "you're gonna crank 'em up again." Nothing had changed.

A few of the younger players were coming in by then. "How's it going?" Scott Loomis said. I told him, "Fine."

Al Ward, a wide receiver who's now in the import-export business, said he had just gone through a divorce. "Well," I said, "if that's what you wanted, congratulations." He said, "Yeah, that's exactly how I feel." Ward also said he had read the stories about me. "You know," he said, "there're a lot of different ways for different people, and I'm realizing that more and more." Sonny laughed: "Hey, I see you've gone public." Jim Lambright, a coach himself now, said, "Well, you're gonna crank 'em up again." He was no different.

I went into the tunnel out to the field and met Martin Wyatt, who had been a great little running back when I played. The last time I had seen him, three years before, he was out of shape and looked terrible. I said, "You really look great compared to the last time I saw you." "Yeah, I dropped about sixty," he said. Martin was then working for a television station and he asked if he could do an interview. We sat at the edge of the field and chatted before the camera.

220

Martin asked if I would do it all over again. I said I would because I felt it was important for somebody to speak out and explain some things about being an athlete, being homosexual. He asked me if Coach Jim Owens would have been outraged by my homosexuality if he had known when I was playing for Washington. "You know," I told him, "people ask me that about Lombardi. I have to say I don't know how he would have reacted. We've made a lot of changes. We've all changed. Back then, we weren't ready for a lot of things we talk about now. I hope the coaches would have thought only about my contributions to the team, but I can't say for sure."

What I know from my own experience is that a lot of coaches and owners already know they have homosexuals playing for them on NFL teams. They're sophisticated enough to know that this isn't going to cause any problems in the locker room. What they're afraid of—and, I think, the only thing they're afraid of—is the publicity about it that might affect box-office receipts. The incredible thing about all this is that nobody really knows, for sure, what the fans think. Personally I don't think most fans really give a damn whether a player is homosexual or not. Even so, most of the coaches and owners and especially the homosexual players themselves still live in terror that the public is going to find out.

Martin Wyatt was now asking me a question that stopped me. "Dave, do you really think those other guys out there want you here?" I thought about it, and finally said, "Martin, I belong here as much as anyone." "Aren't you afraid one of them is going to take a shot at you?" I shrugged and told him no, I could take care of myself on the field. We finished the interview and Martin shook my hand. "You feel free?" he asked. "Yes," I said, "really free."

Dick Wetterauer, who was a guard at Washington when I played there and is now a high school coach, had known about my homosexuality for some time. He said he was glad that I was speaking out about it, that he had changed his own philosophy about coaching. He didn't try to intimidate the players the way our coaches had done to us, but instead tried to make them feel good. "I tell the coaches to say something good first if they're going to chew a kid out. If they can't think of anything else, I tell them to say he looks good in his uniform."

Wetterauer and Harrison Wood (the latter played for Washington 1966-68) were serving as coaches for the Alumni team, and Harrison said, "You know, Dave, the people who're the most uptight about homosexuality are the ones who're most uptight about themselves. They're afraid that if somebody else talks about it they'll find it in themselves."

Rick Redman, the all-American on our team in college who later played for the San Diego Chargers, said to me, "Now you know who your real friends are." I certainly knew he was one. The day after the *Star* interview was published—the day the Eagles coach, Mike McCormack, was denouncing me in Philadelphia—Rick had told the Associated Press: "I've known Dave for a long time without ever discussing his preferences. I knew what they were but they didn't influence my friendship with him. Dave's got his own preference and I've got mine. I'm not going to pass judgment on Dave Kopay about where his preferences lie. I consider him a friend."

I told Rick how much I appreciated his saying that for publication. I asked him if he were going to play in the Alumni game. He said, "Is a fat dog fat?"

After practice Dick Wetterauer came up and said he wanted me to be one of the captains of the Alumni team. I said that might look like I was trying to make a spectacle of myself. Dick said I deserved to be a captain because I would be one of the older alumni playing and most of the team would know me.

It was turning out to be a good homecoming. Nobody made any cracks. My friends were still my friends. I had been afraid they wouldn't let me play, and now they had named me a cocaptain of the team.

Twenty-Nine

AFTER it was over, Kopay seemed to have expected that nothing would happen. Because he was good to people, he always expected they would be good to him. As his roommate at the San Francisco Forty-Niners had said of him, self-confidence was never one of his problems.

But there remains an honest question about whether his old friends and teammates were in fact accepting him and his homosexuality or whether—as one expressed it—they would have accepted him even if he had come back talking about making it with kangaroos. There is no question that Kopay caused a lot of people to think about homosexuality who would have continued to block it out as a freakish condition of people they would never know. But there was no way that Kopay, or even Young, could be certain what these same people who were welcoming him back to the team were saying behind his back. A "fag" can be the "homosexual friend" who has just left the room.

The fact is that during ten days in Seattle, Kopay was not invited out a single night by any of his old buddies. Two or three were having marital problems at the time, which may explain it for them. But what of the others? Ron Medved, who had played running back in tandem with Kopay at Washington and later played for the Philadelphia Eagles, gave this explanation to Young: "Will there ever come a time when Kopay doesn't feel like he has to talk about it?" Young understood his reaction, but also asked him to look at it from Kopay's point of view. He said he had gone through a similar stage and felt it was important not just for friends to know about and accept his homosexuality, but to be able to talk about it in more general conversations as well.

It would seem that the primary basis for the acceptance as a homosexual that Kopay did get from his old buddies was that they were just that—old buddies, comrades in an earlier life and still friends no matter what he had done. Kopay understood that, at the same time wishing it were broader-based but realizing that it wasn't easy for them either. Their reception was a beginning.

He did draw the line, though, at a comparison Johnny O'Brien made. "It was the same thing last year when George Jugum came back and everybody was talking about him. I said he's still my friend no matter what he's done."

George Joseph Jugum, star linebacker at the University of Washington from 1966 to 1968, was briefly on the rosters of the Los Angeles Rams, and of the British Columbia Lions and the Seattle Rangers in the Continental Football League. After failing to make it as a professional football player, his friends say, Jugum was at loose ends back in Seattle. Then on the morning of February 16, 1974, he and a friend were driving around a restaurant drive-in when a seventeen-year-old boy raised his middle finger in an obscene gesture at Jugum. Jugum chased the boy down and stomped him to death. During his trial Jugum said the boy pulled a knife on him and he had acted in self-defense. The jury found Jugum guilty of second-degree murder just before the 1974 Alumni game. Jugum had not played in that game, but he had attended the team party where his former teammates were friendly and supportive of him. Kopay had asked him, "Why did you have to go out and do something like that? To show how tough you are?" Jugum insisted he'd done it in self-defense. "Self-defense!" said Kopay. "George, you're one of the toughest guys around here. You know nobody is going to beat the shit out of you. Look, I've never lost control like that, but there have been plenty of times when I thought I was going to. I think maybe I know a little bit of what you've been going through. Have you ever stopped to consider that you weren't really mad at that kid, that maybe you were taking it out on him when you were really confused about some other things?" Jugum's answer was to insist on his innocence. He said what had happened had come in an impulsive moment of anger and didn't have anything to do with any kind of confusion about who he was. He felt the dead boy was just as much to blame as he was and that his sentence was unjust. Judge Ward Williams of the Washington State Court of Appeals, in upholding Jugum's conviction, said: "There was testimony that Backman [the boy] did not draw a knife at all. But, assuming that he did, there was such a disparity in the physiques of Jugum and Backman that the jury would be justified in determining that Backman could properly use a knife to defend himself." Jugum is currently serving a sentence of up to thirty years with a minimum of fifteen years before he is eligible for parole. In a similar incident in 1976 three high school football players attacked a young man outside a gay bar in Arizona and beat him to death.

Mike Ditka, a former right end and now a coach with the Dallas Cowboys, is quoted in the NFL's own history, *The First 50 Years,* as saying that the off-season is a time of anxiety for football players. He says he is most relaxed when he is actually involved in the sport. "If I'm not getting rid of my energies this way," he says, "it builds up and I blow it off in some way that isn't proper in this society."

Kopay could perhaps understand better than some others the behavior of people like Jugum, but he had no intention of being lumped with them as good old buddies to be forgiven their sins. As he shouted back at Johnny O'Brien when he mentioned Jugum, "There's no comparison between my homosexuality and what he did."

"Well," O'Brien said, "to a lot of people they're just as bad and they're saying the same things behind your back."

225

"In fact," Kopay told him, "being open about my true sexual feelings is the first step toward getting over all that confusion that causes people to be so crazy and violent."

While they were in Seattle, Kopay and Young taped interviews with several of Kopay's teammates. A younger player who is now studying to be a lawyer in Los Angeles had not heard about Kopay's homosexuality. "Jesus, I don't know what to say . . . homosexuality in football? I always thought football was the last bastion of masculinity." Kopay said: "Masculinity? Male homosexuality is pure masculinity." The young man was noticeably cool toward Kopay afterward.

Remarkably, most of the players interviewed—especially those who had gone on to the pros—had carefully considered the negative aspects of the sport. Many of them had been through psychoanalysis themselves and had been forced to examine their own involvement in the game. One said he had loved his wife and children but he had to put football first for so long it was now too late for him to rescue his marriage. Another sat through an hour interview talking about his former teammates as the best of comrades in the best of all possible games. When Young turned off the tape recorder he said, "I don't think I've given you very much." "I just don't believe you," Young said.

"Listen," the player went on, "I have three degrees in myself. I've spent a hundred and fifty hours in psychoanalysis trying to become something besides a former football player. I hope the sport is dying a terminal illness; I hope this is the last game ever played." Whatever he hoped it would be, this former pro football player ran onto the field in the Alumni game and proceeded to play as aggressively as he ever had before.

Another revealing instance of football's hold—no matter what they say—on those who have been in it happened one night when Kopay and Young stopped by at a new restaurant that was built by the water, with tables set out on a pier. Making their way through them they almost stumbled over the table where Rick Sortun was sitting with a date. Sortun, strikingly handsome as a college boy and a star on the same teams Kopay had played on, went on to play several years for the St. Louis Cardinals and was one of the few players mentioned favorably in Dave Meggyesy's *Out of Their League.*

Like Meggyesy, Sortun had ended up embittered about his football experience. But, also like Meggyesy, he had never been able to reconcile his doctrinaire leftist politics with the fact that there had been moments of real enjoyment in the game he now professed to despise. Sortun said, "There is nothing good about football, no excuse for the game," he told Kopay. "Dave Meggyesy is my comrade, but you're only my friend." Then, almost in the next breath, he said, "Why is it I have no friends from football?"

Sortun was too proud to do it, but his date kept saying "please join us" to Kopay and Young. Sortun sat there—his once trim, athletic body now gone to paunch—a very different person from the football buddy Kopay remembered. "I figured a lot of the players would be out tonight," Sortun said. "I wonder where they are."

"Yeah," Kopay said later. "Sortun hates football now, but he's wondering where his teammates are tonight."

Kopay attended the official pre-game team party alone. Coach Jim Owens was there—a businessman now, retired from coaching after several years of disappointing seasons. He looked haggard, older than his years. Kopay had heard that Owens had been shocked by his public disclosures about homosexuality, but at the team party Owens shook hands with Kopay, said, "Hello, how are you?"—no more, no less than he had said in years past. He seemed uneasy and distant—but he always had. There was no way to tell how he really felt—and there never had been.

We had had a really good practice and I was late getting to the party in a downtown hotel. I was still anxious because there would be a lot of people at the party I hadn't seen yet and I was wondering what some of them would be thinking about me and what I was doing.

Most of the people had already filed through the buffet line, but I found four of my old buddies—Ron Medved, Dick Wetterauer, Rick Redman and Johnny O'Brien—together at one table. Everybody was jiving about old times. Redman was telling a story about me and Medved during the California game at Berkeley in 1963. The game was played in 102-degree heat and we just wanted to get it over with. Redman got down like a quarterback and started talking like Bill Douglas, who had been our quarterback. He said all he could hear was me and Ron back there saying "don't give me the ball, don't give me the ball."

Somebody else remembered how hot it had been during the Rose Bowl game. One of the guys came up to a coach complaining of cotton mouth or parched throat. The coach gave him a bottle of analgesic and the poor guy swigged it down.

Johnny O'Brien said, "Let me tell you, Dave, I've really been sticking my neck out for you." I said, "Well, Johnny, I don't want to be causing you problems." He said, "No, I do it 'cause you're my friend and I don't like people talking about you."

O'B said he was the oldest living graduate assistant coach in the country. He also said that at practice the day before one of his young players was mouthing off about how he would like "to take a shot at Kopay." Johnny said he'd stopped the guy and told him, "You better learn how to play a lot better than you do or Kopay'll run right over you."

There is a time at the team party when everybody gets up and tells what he's been doing. One guy said, "I'm still doing what I was doing last year." Another guy said he had just gotten back from Mexico, which was also what he had been doing every year since he left college. Another one said he was still a professional student. I stood up and said, "My name's Dave

Kopay and I'm tired of talking about myself." They cracked up.

O'Brien stood up next. "I'm O'B," he said, "and Kopay's a pretty tough act to follow."

The day of the game I was the first one in the locker room, just as I always had been. We were supposed to be there at 11 a.m., I got there at 10. I had been having some trouble with my ankles and my knee and wanted to have plenty of time to get taped up and see that my equipment fitted just right. Hell, I was thinking, I'm old and I don't want to get hurt. It seemed kind of strange getting fitted out again. I think I knew this would be my last game.

Ben Davidson, who graduated four years before I did and later played defensive end fourteen years for Green Bay, Washington and Oakland, said, "If I break my leg in this game I could lose a helluva lot of money. I don't know what I'm doing here." I told him this was probably my last game. He said, "Well, I'll probably be back next year."

Several guys hit me on the shoulder and said, "Well, this is it." They meant more than the game about to start—they also meant we were about to see how 23,000 people were going to react to me.

Ron Medved said, "Well, you're definitely going to get some kind of reaction out there." Dick Wetterauer laughed and said, "Well, Kopay, once a star always a star." He also thought everything was going great. "Look what's happened this week, there hasn't been one single asshole who has said anything to you." And Dick Aguirre, who played for Washington in 1959–60, said, "Hell, people will have to respect you for having the strength to stand up for who you are."

I suppose it would have been more nostalgic to play in the old stadium, but it was exciting enough in the new King Dome. Before the game the captains always go to the center of the field and toss a coin to see which side will kick and which will receive. Now I looked around and saw that they were doing this in the locker room, and I figured it was because they were afraid there would be some reaction if I went out to represent the Alumni team. I asked Medved about it and he said I was being too sensitive. Nobody ever did explain, though, why the toss wasn't held on the field.

Next would come the introductions, and I stood there on the sidelines wondering what would happen when my number and name were called. Everything had gone just fine that week, but maybe some of the fans would be so outraged they would boo when my name was announced. I heard my number, ran onto the field—and all I could hear was applause.

High up in the stands, Young sat poised with his pen and notebook to record the reaction. There was not a single boo when Kopay's name was first announced or during any of the other times when he was sent in and out of the game. A man behind Young whispered to his companion, "Is that the gay one?" Young moved around to record their comments, but, instead, overheard the oldtimers talking about what a great football player Kopay was.

Maybe the fans had changed too; maybe they really didn't care how a football player had sex. Not long after this, *The San Francisco Chronicle* conducted a sidewalk poll, asking people if they objected to homosexuals playing professional football. Not one of them did. One man said: "That's fine with me. I mean pro football is a job. The job is playing football and there is no sex on the field. It's like driving a bus. You do a job and then go home and close the door."

We ran back to the sidelines and one of my teammates glanced at me and said, "Well, that's over with." They started a young running back ahead of me, but that was no problem for me. I got in for a few plays and it felt good.

I could also feel the years. My knee was bothering me and I

had to admit that football was a young man's game. In my life, I knew, it was done, completed. I didn't want to get hurt anymore. I had played my last game.

For the record, the Varsity beat us 10 to 7, but this was one game where winning definitely wasn't the most important thing. A number of reporters crowded around as we were heading toward the buses after the game, but the only thing I said was that Sonny Sixkiller was definitely a professional quality quarterback, that he had played a helluva game and it was a shame he hadn't been signed on by a professional team.

There was a team dinner that night and I went alone as I had for several years. The same group of us sat together as we had for years. We told the same stories we had for years. It seemed that nothing had changed in the way they regarded me, but I had changed and my own self-respect had grown in ways none of them would ever know or understand.

Thirty

THE day after the Alumni game, Sunday, was the day of Kopay's speech to the Dorian Group. It had seemed important to Kopay to have a typed speech; it was a status achievement he felt his parents would appreciate. Young pieced together several of the comments Kopay had made on the talk shows and in newspaper interviews and at a seminar of the Southeastern Gay Conference at the University of North Carolina at Chapel Hill. Charles Brydon retyped the speech in his office and Xeroxed some copies for the press.

Kopay read the speech haltingly, nervously. He had given dozens of speeches at sports banquets during his career, but those had had little to do with his real thoughts. Also, the audience was not as immediately accepting of Kopay as one might have expected. They held back, suspicious of somebody who had been so successful as an athlete, who was—by appearance—so easily accepted in the larger heterosexual society. Nobody had ever called him sissy. How could he understand what they had suffered through?

But when Kopay began to speak—softly, stumbling in his effort to make the words express his true feelings, and clearly scared, the audience could begin to identify. In his life, he said, he had known their same fears and confusions. The stereotypes about athletes were just as unjust as the stereotypes about homosexuals. When he had finished, he looked up and said, "Thank you." The audience gave him a standing ovation, then crowded around him, more comfortable with him now, and talked to him easily. Among them were doctors and teachers and reporters and waiters and students. There was a member of the 1972 Canadian Olympic team who offered his support. An English teacher came up to Young and asked if it was his idea to include a poem by Kay Boyle in the speech. "Absolutely not," Young said. "Kopay read it and wanted to read it in the speech." And then a young actor was baiting Kopay about who had actually written the speech, or rather he was asking leading questions suggesting Kopay hadn't done it himself. Young said: "Listen, why don't you say what you mean?" The young actor backed off.

Afterward, as Kopay and Young were going up the walkway to Brydon's house, Kopay put his arm around Young and laughed. " 'Why don't you say what you mean?' The fucker didn't think a dumb jock could write his own speech."

And by the way, Kopay said, he had checked on those flowers. Begonias didn't die in the winter. The blooms died but the plants live year-round. "Okay," Young said, "show me one of your begonias." Kopay walked straight to a bright purple rhododendron, which Young identified for him. The two grabbed each other and laughed. "The Dodgers won ten in a row," Young said.

The next day after the speech, all of the radio and television stations and newspapers in the area were represented at the press conference in Brydon's office. Georg N. Meyers, sports editor of *The Seattle Times*, who had been such a fan of Kopay's when he was a college and professional ball player, was among them. Meyers wrote: "Shortly after the Forty-Niners signed Kopay as a free agent I chatted in passing with Jack Christiansen, the head coach, and asked about Kopay's chances. 'I don't know how,' said Christiansen, 'but I think he'll make it.' Kopay made it in football. This time it may be tougher."

After the press conference, Kopay met with Mayor Wes Uhlman in his office. This was only a few weeks after the Supreme Court ruling that upheld the right of states to make laws against private sexual acts between consenting adults. Uhlman said he was afraid the Supreme Court ruling would set off a wave of lower court rulings and the mood of the legislatures would swing against revision of the laws. He also said it might be popular for him to come out for the rights of homosexuals in Seattle, but it would never do in Tacoma or Yakima.

Kopay reminded him that Seattle wasn't the only place where homosexuals lived in the state of Washington. An assistant then came in to tell the mayor he had another appointment, but he waved him aside and continued on with Kopay, who talked of the fact that he was not the only homosexual among professional football players and reminded the mayor that there were homosexuals in every place and stratum of our society. Whether this conversation was the cause of it or not, the mayor afterward spoke out—as few candidates ever have in America—in favor of legal rights for homosexuals.

Leaving Seattle was a relief after ten busy, tension-packed days. Kopay and Young had dinner at the restaurant on top of the Space Needle and then left early the next morning, feeling good about getting on with the trip.

Kopay's brother Tony was the next person on the list of confrontations. Tony Kopay worked as an assistant coach at Oregon State University in Corvallis, Oregon, just a few hours by interstate highway due south from Seattle.

This meeting was so difficult for Kopay he still can't talk about it without crying. Obviously his relationship with his brother was far more complicated than Young could have understood. Kopay was visibly anxious as they turned off the interstate highway and headed toward Corvallis. Young was thinking only of meeting up with an old college friend.

Kopay was choked up and angry as they pulled into the newspaper's parking lot to meet Young's friend. He didn't want any reporters around because he didn't want to risk embarrassing his brother on his own turf. Finally Kopay registered at a motel and learned that his brother was already staying there, having taken a room until his new house was

234

finished and his family could join him from Missouri. He had not called ahead and didn't know, for certain, that his brother would even be there.

Thirty-One

I WENT on up to my room alone and Perry Young went off to his friend's house. I left a message at the motel desk, telling Tony what room I was staying in and asking him to call when he came in.

I also called the coaches' office at the university. I left a message the first time I called, but after an hour Tony still hadn't called me back. I called a second time and talked with a young coach who seemed very friendly. He said he had followed my career for several years and we chatted on about football. He assured me that Tony was there that day and he had received my messages to call.

After three hours I gave up waiting, called Perry and went to dinner with him and his friend. At the restaurant the friend asked me, "How did it go with your brother?" I tried to speak. I couldn't. I went outside and cried.

I guess I had spent my life up through college chasing after Tony, and even after I made it in the pros I was still looking back for his approval. When I first told him, privately, about my homosexuality, he hadn't seemed upset. In fact his calm understanding was a real help to me. There was nobody whose respect I wanted more than his and when it mattered most he had been there to support me.

Then he had turned on me in a way I just never expected or could be prepared for. He had been ruined, he said, because of my public discussion of homosexuality. He blamed me for losing out on the head coaching job at Oregon State. I know that Tony is a fine coach, and that he was among those in the final running for the head coaching job. I also realize that if he were a borderline case anything might influence the decision about hiring him. Maybe I'm trying to relieve my guilt by mentioning this, but everybody I'd talked to said that Craig Fertig had the inside track on the head coaching job from the start. As soon as Fertig was named head coach he named Tony his top assistant.

Anyway it seemed a little unfair—or maybe the word is "inaccurate"—for Tony to lay all the blame on me, and to think entirely of himself when I couldn't get a job even as a scout or an assistant coach. But in fact we hadn't talked about any of this. Everything I had heard about him had been relayed to me by my mother and sister.

After dinner that night I went off by myself to a bar, where a young student recognized me and introduced himself. He talked freely about his sexuality. It was no problem to him and I had a feeling that he was like most of the students in college these days.

Back at the motel there were no messages from my brother. It was too late, I felt, to call him, so I went to bed. I wasn't at all prepared to see him when he came by the next morning. It was very early and I was hung over and he looked like he had also had a rough night.

I asked him if he had been out drinking after practice the day before and he said yes. "You mean you didn't get any of my messages?" No. I went in and brushed my teeth and combed my hair. I was still feeling rotten.

And it was not just from the after effects of booze. Confronting Tony, and his disapproval, was bringing to a head years and years of guilty feelings. My brother Tony was not just a brother to me—he was coach, priest, father figure too. His rejection of my homosexuality was a rejection of me. It was the world saying to me again that I was somehow unfit because my sexual feelings were for my own sex.

Worse, he had not only judged me unfit, he had also said my being open about who I was had hurt his career. The night after the *Star* interview was published he had called my parents to tell them what he felt I had done to him.

Sitting there trying to explain myself to Tony, I had never felt so isolated, alone, and angry. Why should I be sitting there having to justify my life? Tony didn't have to justify his life.

I had left him some articles—not just about me but the whole subject of homosexuality—at the motel desk. He said he hadn't even looked at them, which made me even madder. At one point he said, "I'll pray for you," and I told him, "That's not what it's all about." "But I want to pray for you." "I don't want your prayers," I said. And all the while he kept saying, "I just can't accept it."

I didn't remind him that he had behaved differently when I first told him, before I went public, but I did ask him if anybody had made any cracks to him about me. He said, "No, but it's been really hard for me, really hard." "Tony," I told him, "you're a good coach and you'll be given credit for that. Don't go out there and try to be some kind of tough guy just because everybody knows your brother's a homosexual." I told him about the student who had talked to me in the bar the night before. I told him that I believed people were changing, that I was sure his players would see right through him if he tried to put on a tough act.

"Accept" was what Tony had said he couldn't do for me. And it was a key word—then and now. Wanting him— people—to accept me had everything to do with why I was so upset, and still am at the memory of that morning. Tony's opinion is important to me. I want to be taken seriously. I want to be honest about who I am. I don't want to be thought of as some freak, I want to be considered a whole person.

After we had talked for a while longer in my room Tony said he wanted to show me the house he was building and drove me out to a subdivision of expensive new homes for upper-echelon university officials. By then we were both more relaxed, and he introduced me to all the men who were working for him.

Afterward he drove me back to the motel, and we said our

238

good-byes—almost formally. We both knew it would be a long time before we saw each other again. I told myself that at least I had confronted him, but I also knew that he and I hadn't really faced up to what now separated us. I don't think either of us was changed by this meeting in Corvallis.

Thirty-Two

KOPAY'S younger brother Gary and his family lived in Hollister, California, just south of San Francisco. Again, Kopay had not called ahead. He and Young stopped in San Jose, where he called to see if his brother was home. Young had said he could stay in a motel if there were any problems with his brother. Then they both stopped— maybe they were creating problems that didn't exist. Brother Gary invited them both to dinner and insisted they stay the night.

Gary and Charla Kopay had built a spacious house in a subdivision around a new golf course, surrounded by miles and miles of cultivated fields, with signs advertising everything from artichokes to apricots. Gary came out to welcome them with warm smiles and handshakes while Charla, who had lived in Japan for two years, was busy preparing a special dinner of beef teriyaki.

Kopay seemed especially comfortable with them—a feeling that was immediately shared by Young. Gary took them into the backyard, where he had just put up a wide-board fence and was starting to lay out a garden that would include a fish pool.

There was a remarkable contrast between the meetings with the two brothers. With Gary, Kopay had none of the fear-ridden anxiety and real anger he had expressed before and after his meeting with Tony. He was comfortable, at ease with his younger brother and his family.

Kopay started to show the articles about himself and homosexuality, but Gary said, "I don't need to read any of that, it's just not a consideration in my life." He said that after the interview with David was published nationwide he had gotten a frantic call from his father. The elder Kopay had asked if he were "ready for a bomb," then told him about the interview and Tony's report that he was ruined as a coach because of it. Gary had helped to calm his father and Tony—the first time he had talked to Tony in three years. He had told them that he felt David had a right to do whatever he wanted, that it shouldn't affect anybody else, and didn't justify the way they were carrying on.

After the call, Gary had reported the news to his supervisor at the telephone company, who told him not to worry, that his brother's sexual orientation was no problem to them.

Apparently Gary had made up his mind about David's homosexuality and people's reaction to it just as he had made up his mind about the Catholic Church—the old attitudes didn't make sense to him, and they were not going to affect his life.

It was difficult to imagine Gary as a 99-pound weakling. Now he stood more than six feet, weighed more than 200 pounds. He had grown in other ways too. Here he was, once the pale shadow of his football hero brothers, obviously stronger and in far better control of his life and feelings than either of them. He criticized David for being so emotional when he tried to talk with their parents. His crying made them cry, and that wasn't doing any good for anybody. He suggested that David be just as direct with them as he had been. "Go in there and say, 'Look, this is the way it's going to be. Take it or leave it.'"

Gary's two young daughters are spirited and free in a way their father and uncle couldn't be. They get a voice in the decisions about their lives; they don't live by rigid schedules; they do live with constant physical affection from both parents.

The next morning Kopay and Young exchanged warm good-byes with Gary and Charla and the two girls and set off across the mountains, through Salinas and south toward Los Angeles—and the final confrontation.

It is one kind of courage to face millions of people through the impersonal technology of television, quite another to meet face-to-face with just two, who happen to be your parents.

In Los Angeles Kopay and Young both had friends to look up, so there were plausible excuses for putting off the final meeting with Kopay's parents.

One afternoon, still marking time, they took the San Diego Freeway south of Compton, where Kopay had to stop and ask directions—he had not been to the seminary on Dominguez Hill since he was a high school student. The area had become a sprawling industrial complex. There were no farms or open fields visible in any direction.

The first view of the seminary campus was obscured by a new freeway intersection. The first gates they came to were locked; the second ones bore a marker designating this as a California Historic Site.

Kopay could sense the change immediately. There was the huge purple bougainvillea where it had always been, but the grounds themselves were shaggy, unkempt. There were no cars and no signs of life. Finally they spotted a painter, working quietly on the porch of the old Dominguez ranch house, who told them the place was locked but there might be somebody who could give them some information in the office of the other building.

Just then a middle-aged woman pulled up in a car as they were walking across to the main seminary building. She asked if she could help. When Kopay told her he had been a student there she asked, "Oh, when were you here?" He told her the years and she said, "Oh, that was when Father Tomasich was here." "Is he still here?" Kopay asked. "Oh no," she said, "he's out." Did she mean out of the seminary? "Oh, no, he's all the way out. He got married."

They went on into the office and looked up Kopay's file—a stiff white card full of letters and numbers that recorded only that he had been a good student, well-behaved, and nothing more. The woman said that the priest in charge of the place was out. She acted as if the place were still in use.

Kopay and Young then took the narrow paved road up the hill to the junior seminary buildings. Kopay gasped at the sight of the place. A statue of Jesus stared out from a tangle of weeds, chunks of paint were peeling off the face and arms. The lawns were almost knee-high in uncut grass and weeds. The rows of ligustrum and gardenias near the buildings were out of shape and dying. Rusted chains with padlocks held the sagging doors of the main entrance together. Inside, they could see that the place had been abandoned in shambles. One door opened onto a room cluttered with books and religious texts. The seated figure of Pius XII—arm raised in benediction—looked up from a broken frame in the rubble.

Huge tumbleweeds, six feet across, had ambled into the courtyards, where bedsprings and rotted couches were piled against the walls. The paved basketball courts had weeds growing up shoulder high from between the cracks as Kopay moved to center court, pantomiming a jump-hook shot.

The sprinkler system, which Kopay had helped to install as a student, had been left on behind the buildings, and in a damp clump there Young stumbled on a pocket-size copy of *The Mirror*, the strict code of behavior Kopay had lived under at the seminary.

They found an open window and climbed in. The chapel looked as if it had never been used—the terrazzo floors were still shining—but vandals had sprayed their names on many of the walls. In one room, somebody had written: "God was here but he left."

Kopay was smiling as he led Young down one of the stark hallways toward the room where he had slept. "Oh, you should have seen us sashaying along with our robes flying out." Young was puzzled by Kopay's banter. Kopay had seemed such a hyper-emotional person about everything else in his past, and here he was in a setting that should have

243

evoked much of the anguish of his early sexual feelings and the way, he said, the church had made him feel about them. Maybe it was like soldiers coming on a shrine desecrated by war. All that had inspired awe in the place was now gone.

Would Kopay have behaved differently if the place had been full of believers? "No," Kopay said, "I just don't feel anything about all of this now. I'm the one who's changed."

There had been an earlier experience when Kopay had cried in a religious setting. He and Young had stopped by to hear a sermon by Young's older brother, who is the Methodist chaplain at Duke University. The service—featuring music from a $500,000 organ and a choir the size of most congregations—was in the huge gothic chapel that towers above the campus around it. After the sermon, Kopay sat there crying, and they sat in the gardens outside for a long time without speaking. Finally Young said, "You were crying because your religion is still a part of you. The procession, the liturgy and the music all must have reminded you of that gap in your life now."

"No," Kopay said. "You're wrong. I was thinking of his sermon and how sad it is that all those people still believe that stuff." The text of the sermon was the scripture about Abraham getting the message from God to kill his son. The story of the biblical father and son seemed to remind Kopay of his own parents' relationship with the church, God, and their relationship with him. His parents had accepted the dictates of the church without question. And these included this story in which a father is glorified for his willingness to kill his only son to please his God. They also included a fixed belief that homosexuality is perverse and evil, a mortal sin against the will of God. By rejecting their son's homosexuality—and thereby him—they were only obeying the will of their god. They surely felt their sacrifice would be rewarded—as did Abraham.

They had now been in Los Angeles for several days. It was the day before they had planned to leave, and Kopay still had not spoken with his parents—even though he knew his sister Marguerite was visiting them. He told Young that he might not go through with it. Young told him he had to, and not just for the book.

That morning they drove out to Kopay's high school and talked with one of the brothers who had been Kopay's teacher. He was courteous, but Kopay's public talk about homosexuality was not mentioned. Outside, a young coach was barking orders to some students, and Kopay smiled at the memory of himself in their shoes.

Riding around the neighborhood, Kopay kept talking about maybe not going to see his parents, about what, if he did go, he was supposed to do, or say. "Do your really want a sermon?" Young asked. Kopay said he did.

"Okay. You've come this far. You've come through all the others. Use the strength and integrity I know you've got. Always before, you got so emotional they thought your life was nothing but the worst kind of misery. You say that most of what's happened to you has been for the good and that you've learned to enjoy it. All right, tell them about that. Go tell them how you honestly feel, that homosexuality is no longer a problem in your life and you wish it wouldn't be in theirs. Don't try to convert them. Just speak up for yourself."

Kopay drove off to face his parents alone.

Thirty-Three

I WENT around back and said hello to Dad. He keeps saying each year that he's not going to have a garden, but every year he plants one. The tomatoes and onions and leaf lettuce and peppers and carrots and corn were as healthy as always and he was proud to show them to me.

I told him I needed to get some stuff that was stored in the garage. He made a joke about being in the moving and storage business. He asked about the game in Seattle, about Johnny O'Brien and Rick Redman and some others he had met from those days. I went on into the house, but I couldn't find mother. I was thinking, oh my God, she's hiding.

But she was in the bathroom primping. I met her in the den and she gave me a big hug. She was trying hard to keep her composure—and she did. So did I. I said, "Well, what's for dinner?" carrying on an old joke from the days when they thought of me as a visiting garbage man because I would eat any and all leftovers. She said I had missed a big turkey dinner the week before. I said maybe next time.

She said, "Will you stay for dinner tonight?" I said I didn't know I was invited. She said, "Of course you are."

Mother asked about the book and the guy I was writing it with. She said they had put the house up for sale and didn't let me forget that I was the reason they were having to do it. (When they sold the house they got three times the amount they paid for it.) They were going to move up to Sacramento to be near Gary and his family.

Marguerite said she thought this would work out to be the best thing that could have happened to them, that otherwise

246

they would never have made a change. She also said she had never enjoyed a visit home as much as this one. She hadn't been out by herself a single night, she had been happy to stay home with mother and dad. "All of this," she said, had brought them closer together. In fact, she had never seen them so loving and considerate with each other.

Of course I know this has something to do with their sharing what they consider a "burden." But I like to think it also has led them to think about a lot of their old attitudes they never questioned before, and that along the way they've maybe taken a new look at their own relationship so that they can begin to live without so much friction, with a little more love and understanding.

After dinner Marguerite and I went to the Studio One, a gay discotheque just off Santa Monica Boulevard near Beverly Hills. It's a huge place, the size of a warehouse. Marguerite had never been to a gay bar before, but she and I laughed and hugged and danced for a long time.

She said she had never had so much fun in a bar. As we were saying good-bye, she said, "This has been good for me too, David. Please come back, come home whenever you will."

I drove away from Los Angeles leaving behind a lifetime of hypocrisy and shame. It was all out in the open now and I had faced up, as best I could, to every one of them.

It's a new life for me now—without football, living openly as a homosexual. But I'm facing it with the strength of an honest man. And that's got to be a good beginning.